WHY WAS I GOING BACK? ...

The truth was there were hidden fears gnawing
at me, fears I had no idea how to face, but that
had to be faced sometime. I knew I would never
be able to move forward, to build on whatever
I had achieved, for myself, for others, for Lucy,
for James, unless I faced them.

I had never imagined the road to recovery
would be so long, or that it would ever lead me
back to a wind-whipped shore eight and a half
thousand miles away.

But the time had come.

I had to go back to the Falklands.

SIMON WESTON

Going Back

SIGNET

SIGNET

Published by the Penguin Group
Penguin Books Ltd, 27 Wrights Lane, London W8 5TZ, England
Penguin Books USA Inc., 375 Hudson Street, New York, New York 10014, USA
Penguin Books Australia Ltd, Ringwood, Victoria, Australia
Penguin Books Canada Ltd, 10 Alcorn Avenue, Toronto, Ontario, Canada M4V 3B2
Penguin Books (NZ) Ltd, 182–190 Wairau Road, Auckland 10, New Zealand

Penguin Books Ltd, Registered Offices: Harmondsworth, Middlesex, England

First published by Bloomsbury 1992
Published in Signet 1993
1 3 5 7 9 10 8 6 4 2

John Man is the author of *The Survival of Jan Little* and *The Waorani:
Jungle Nomads of Ecuador* and co-author, with Pin Yathay, of *Stay Alive, My Son*

PICTURE SOURCES
David Thorpe/*News of the World*: pages 1, 2, 3, 4 *bottom*, 5 *bottom*, 6, 7, 8
Press Association: page 5 *top*

Maps on pages 44 and 94 by Neil Hyslop

Printed in England by Clays Ltd, St Ives plc

To my lovely wife, Lucy, and to Mam,
for understanding and not fudging.
I love you both.

ACKNOWLEDGEMENTS

My grateful thanks to Gary and John for their unfailing support and wonderful sense of humour, both on the visit and on our return from the Falkland Islands.

To Malcolm Brinkworth I give my sincere and affectionate gratitude, because without him this meeting would never have taken place. Thanks, mate.

CONTENTS

1

I HAD TO GO BACK

September 1991

The first I knew that something was happening was when Lucy nudged me awake.

'Simon, rub my back,' she said, with a sigh of pain.

'Do you think this is it?' I asked, blearily. It was 3.30 a.m.

'I don't know,' she said, as I got to work. 'It's never happened to me before.'

She was late starting labour, so there'd been plenty of warning. The bags were all packed. To be on the safe side she phoned the midwife, while I took a shower.

Just as well – by the time the midwife arrived, half an hour later, Lucy was getting real pains. We were off, through a soft summer dawn – it was 29 July – to Caerphilly Miners' Hospital, and straight into Delivery.

After Lucy had changed and had an examination, the midwife said it could be a few hours yet. A few hours! Lucy had suffered quite enough already. I wanted things to get a move on. My nerves were shot to pieces, so I went out to get a cup of tea. In one of the corridors I was surprised to meet a member of staff who had once been a military nurse and knew several people who had treated me after the fire. That helped pass some time.

Back in the ward with Lucy, they said things were coming along nicely. God, it was hot in there. Lucy was doing her breathing, grabbing lungfuls of gas and air, not saying anything, just concentrating, while I stood beside her, stroking her forehead, glancing occasionally out of the uncurtained windows, watching the light strengthen over the bushes and trees in the hospital gardens. The doctor came in, a soft-spoken Asian lady who kept Lucy informed of progress.

Suddenly – in a restrained and ladylike voice – Lucy swore, and grabbed me round the neck. The baby's head had started to crown. Then her hand shifted to my chest and grabbed my shirt. All of a sudden I seemed to have no chest hairs left. This was major pain time, and not just for Lucy.

Inside, too, I was all knotted up. I'd heard all the horror stories about what can go wrong. I was as worried as anyone else about whether the baby would be normal or not. On top of that, I had my own special worries. One part of me knew there was no way my genes could have been affected by the bomb, no way that my scars would reappear on my baby's face. But logic had nothing to do with it. There was another part of me that feared the worst.

And I was in fits wondering whether it was going to be a boy or a girl. I really wanted a son, at least the first time around. The idea of a daughter left me feeling very insecure. I felt I could cope with a son, someone to pass on my own experiences to, someone to encourage on the rugby field.

I glanced down. It wasn't as easy as I'd hoped. The doctor was using forceps. There was the head now, and then the back, all bloody, and Lucy's hand was beating at my chest and throttling me, and then the little bum looking like a twin-cheeked chocolate éclair, because the baby's bowels were obviously in fine working order, and then, as the little thing slid round . . .

A boy.

I tried to tell Lucy, but found I couldn't speak at all. It was the matron who said, 'Oh, you've got a boy,' as she lifted him to clean him up.

Lucy was relaxing at last, groggy with the effort and the gas. 'It's a boy,' she said softly, and then kept on repeating, 'It's a boy. It's a boy.'

The matron handed him to me. He was perfect, from his damp fuzz of hair down to his wrinkled feet and button toes.

And I still couldn't talk.

I'm not someone who's usually lost for words, but I *couldn't say a word*. My mouth was opening and closing like a goldfish, my eyes were full of tears, and there was a lump in my throat the size of a beach-ball.

People who say childbirth is the most beautiful thing they've ever seen must be sick, honestly. The sight! The pain that she went through! God! No way in this world would I ever go through anything like that! Yet it was one of the most amazing and wonderful events I've ever witnessed. I wouldn't have missed it for the world, and if we are lucky enough to have more children, I won't miss their births either.

Standing there, holding James, with tears blurring the sight of him, was the most moving experience I'd had since I got injured. It had been nine years since an Argentinian bomb had blown away my old life, along with almost half my skin; nine years in which I had been patched back together, recuperated, left the Army, travelled, done things I would never have dreamed of, discovered the rewards of helping others as I had been helped, become a husband and, now, been given the joy of becoming a father.

James was a seal set on a new life.

You'd think I'd have been all set to live happily ever after. I was grateful, don't get me wrong; if this was all there was to life, it was OK by me. But there was something missing, a restlessness that I felt in still moments, a hidden unhappiness revealed by the nightmares that still occasionally came at me, something that had to be explored. I knew I wouldn't be able to do my best by Lucy and James unless I found out what it was, and coped with it.

Superficially, of course, in body and mind I was in great shape, compared with the mess I'd been in when I emerged from hospital in 1983. I still have a rebuilt nose and a moustache that won't grow straight, a face like a badly-chewed pasty (in the words of one of my closest friends) and a head that looks as if I've just been scalped. It always makes me smile when I have a haircut and the barber politely shows me the back of my head in the mirror. There's no hair there at all, because the skin came from some other part of my body and it's as tender as a baby's. If it gets exposed to the sun by mistake, it turns an instant tomato-red.

But at least I *have* a face – not all that pretty, but one I've become used to, which is why I can joke about it, and why it's good for friends to joke about it, too. I don't want you to think it was an easy journey, though, as anyone who has a facial injury – especially a burn – will tell you. Face and hands – these are the bits that really define you as an individual in the eyes of other people, the bits that everyone notices, that can't be covered up. It was a long hard struggle to accept that the face staring at me from the mirror was not a mask hiding the real Simon Weston, but *part of* the real Simon Weston, the new me. What you see is what you get. People stare, but it doesn't bother me now. If they don't like the way I look, that's their problem.

For years there hadn't been much more to improve on, except the middle finger of my left hand, and even that was in better shape now.

My hands had become a mess in the few seconds after the bomb, when I grabbed one of the lads who was on fire. The left hand was the worse of the two. The little finger had been burned off and the others were badly distorted. The middle finger was bent over backwards and twisted, and was always getting in the way. So at the end of 1989 they decided to operate. It may sound only a small thing after what I'd been through, but it hurt like hell. In fact, at the time I thought it was the most painful operation I'd had, probably because I'd forgotten a lot of the suffering and because I wasn't used to it. They broke the finger and shoved a pin up it to keep it straight. It swelled up and got infected, and gave me the most excruciating pain for about four weeks.

But that was over now. So physically I was about as perfect as I'd ever be. Well, to be honest, I was a bit overweight, but that's never a major worry with me because I'll always have my prop-forward build and I can always weight-train and run my way to fitness if I want to.

Emotionally, too, I had come a long way. Once, I'd been a happy-go-lucky squaddie whose main ambition in life was to fill in my pools coupons every Friday. The fire burned away all that. For a while afterwards I felt as though I had been left with nothing, and I sank into depression and drink. Slowly, with a lot of medical and psychiatric help, I emerged.

In all this I was lucky – lucky to have survived, lucky to have the help I did. Even the *Sir Galahad* incident itself had its lucky side, though it took me a long time to see it. It gave me a unique opportunity to change. I decided I didn't much like the person I had been before. I could do better.

When I joined the Army, I joined to see the world, to fire a gun, to wear a uniform. I was nothing but a big kid, thinking only of myself and the next pay cheque. It was like going from one school to another, to a school uniform with pay. We could jump in the mud, drink, do all the things mothers disapprove of, get fit, play sport, get paid, eat, always have a bed to go to at night, get paid, have a beer, get paid, have friends, get *paid* – for being in uniform, can you believe it? For being like a big kid (albeit a professional one)!

Because you have to have a certain childish mentality to be in the armed forces, especially in Northern Ireland, where we felt we could do with all the laughs we could get. Once, Tommy 'Mad Mo' Morris put on an NBC (nuclear, chemical and biological suit), installed himself in the pit beneath the 'thunderbox', the six-holes-in-a-plank toilet, and ignited a thunderflash. Boom! Six bare-arsed squaddies tore out into the field, swearing they'd never eat Army curry again. That, I'm sorry to say, was high-level humour by Army standards.

And the discipline! Just like school. At school you get told off for having dirt on your blazer or your tie undone. It's no different in the Army. The only difference is that in the Army they fine you rather than give you lines.

When I got injured, my life changed at a stroke. The bomb wiped out the life I'd had before. In the Army, at least I'd been a kid. After the fire, I became a baby again, totally dependent on others. I couldn't eat, move, even relieve myself, without the help of others. Outwardly – physically – the best I could look forward to was being someone totally different. There was no help for it: I had to change inwardly as well. I resisted, of course. But as time passed I saw that there was a way to gain some benefit from what had happened. I had been given an opportunity not many people get. Because I looked different, nobody was going to stop me from acting differently. There were no expectations to fulfil. I could be a different person. In metamorphosis, I could, with luck, find liberation (big words for a Welsh squaddie, but that was part of the change, too).

So if my time in the Army extended my childhood, the injury was the beginning of a different sort of growing up. I can imagine more comfortable ways of growing up. If I could have had the choice of being injured or not, I would never have been injured. But since I *was* injured, things couldn't have gone better. I gained the courage to show myself in public. I started to work with charities. I was the subject of three television documentaries, and wrote a book about my recovery, *Walking Tall*.

I owe part of the change in my life to public exposure. It wasn't my idea, but I'll always be grateful for the way the documentaries and the book forced me to change, to grow in confidence. For months after the injury, I could do nothing at all except talk. That was an education in itself. Then later, for the book, which was 'ghosted' from my tapes, I spoke for the first time about the fire on the *Sir Galahad*. It meant reviving bitter, horrible memories, but it was also a release. I began to let go of the past, and it began to let go of me.

The response from the public was the best medicine anyone could have, an inspiration, repeated hundreds of times. People said I'd given them the strength to face tragedy, but their courage strengthened me in return. The letters amazed me – thousands of them, bag-loads of them, some from people eager for me to turn to religion (one was even signed 'Jesus'), but most from ordinary people who'd been feeling bad about themselves, or about something that had happened in their lives. It was good to know that my survival allowed them to see there could be a way forward.

I'll let one letter stand for hundreds, one that I find particularly moving, not just for what it says but for what it leaves out:

6 June 1985

Dear Simon,

Thank you for allowing us to meet you in your television series and the magazine article. You not only went to protect us in the Falklands as a soldier . . . but you saved two people this week.

My youngest daughter and I thought that we had to end our intolerable situation, which has lasted for four years, but much, much longer in a lesser degree.

As we discussed our plan, *Simon's War* came on the TV. We did not sleep that night. No one – not even two other daughters and two grandchildren – was able to do for us what you have done: made us realize that we have to live, and not only that – be brave and positive, and keep going, and stop the luxury of our self-pity.

We know it will not be easy: but with you out there, your terrific spirit, your humanity, you are our talisman.

The way back for us in trying to become human beings again is to think of others apart from ourselves, and we will think of you, Simon, and concentrate on your well-being, your future, because you are worthwhile.

We wept for you, and with you (I know it sounds trite, but it is true). If only we could have helped you and your dear mum and dad, but we didn't know. Now that we do, our lives have been changed. Your destiny altered ours. Thank you and God bless you.

I knew my role in their new-found courage must have been marginal. The spirit must have been there in the first place for my experiences to bring it out. I didn't believe I was anything special, and I don't now. But even one letter like that would have been enough to make me think I was doing something right. I couldn't help feeling a new sense of responsibility to those in physical or emotional need.

The reactions never stopped amazing me. One man on holiday in Spain said proudly that it had taken him three days to read the book – and it was the first book he'd read all the way through. Friends who heard me on the radio and television accused me of taking elocution lessons. I began to reassess myself, and the experience gave me a sense of new-found freedom. I felt as if I'd been lobotomized at birth and somebody had just given me my frontal lobes back.

Of course, it wasn't all down to me. The press played an important part. I've never really understood why they focused on me, but I was working for charity a good deal, and perhaps that made it easy for people to like me. Anyway, to be fair, as much as the press have been bad to other people, to me they've been brilliant. Without the press, I'd be a nobody, and a lot of deserving charity cases would be worse off.

The response to going public confirmed me in my decision to get involved in charity work. It wasn't a simple decision. When I first got injured I didn't want anything to do with it, because I suppose I felt I was a charity case myself. It's a hard thing to face up to the fact that you're disabled, especially when you're twenty-one, all strength and vitality and rugby and beer. I certainly didn't want to admit that I was a part of what a lot of charities are set up for, and that I might remain so, for ever.

It was only when PHAB – Physically Handicapped and Able Bodied – in Devon approached me that I began to see that I could do some good. They don't ask me to do too much now, but whenever they do, I'll help if I can, because through them I stopped being a charity case myself. They hold a special place in my heart.

The other charity I will always feel close to is the one named after me, the Weston Spirit, set up to encourage and enable young people to overcome adversity within their inner-city environments. Our office was in Liverpool, based in the MCVS (Merseyside Council for Voluntary Services). It was a terrific boost to the charity, and to me personally, when Prince Andrew agreed to sponsor us. He even came to Merseyside, to the pools company Vernons, who had agreed to provide work experience for our youngsters. He flew up from the West Country by helicopter, after half a dozen other engagements, gave a twenty-minute speech and showed he was interested, friendly and well-informed. I was just amazed at the quality of what he gave us – and all while he was on leave from the Navy. How he managed it I don't know, but I'll always be grateful.

Through PHAB and the Weston Spirit, I came to see that by using publicity I could get across a simple message, one it had taken a long time for me to learn (thanks again, Mam), but one that had really helped me when I finally did learn it. If I had to sum it up, it would come down to two words: be positive. If you're not positive, you're never going to get anywhere. People are often too ready to blame lack of achievement on lack of money, on the lack of other people giving them something, instead of creating something for themselves. People who do that sometimes miss the whole point of being alive.

I also happen to believe that sport can play a crucial role in the creation of a positive attitude. I'm biased, of course, because I enjoy sport so much. I think that if young people took part in sport to vent their aggression, they'd be a lot less likely to get involved in trouble. It's not a matter of expense. Youth clubs and councils will usually provide if only . . . OK, this is not the place for a speech, but I do feel strongly about it.

I remember one occasion that really summed up the benefits of this approach to me. Lucy and I were at a running track in Blackpool, presenting prizes at the annual meeting of the Sports Association for the Disabled. In the 100 metres there was one little girl with cerebral palsy who could not co-ordinate her limbs well enough to run. She set off, arms and legs everywhere, obviously excited by the race and the challenge. Within a few paces she fell over. I thought that was it for her, but she got up and continued, and I saw she was laughing. Then she fell over again, and got up again – and again, and again, at least ten times, and every time she did it she laughed, and nothing in this catalogue of failure held her back from her goal, the tape. I watched, enthralled, gripped by a whole spectrum of emotions – wanting to cry, wanting to laugh, wanting to rush out and carry her, wanting to run with her. At last, alone, way behind everyone else, she made it, triumphant. She had won her own personal race. That, I thought, was how I had to live my life.

It works both ways. I get back as much as I give. Every now and then, something happens to remind me that I have this link with thousands of people I'll never know. Once, in an Indian restaurant, a drunken Scotsman behind me started to throw punches at waiters who were trying to ease him out. He was so Brahms and Liszt that a few of his punches landed on my shoulders and spilled curry down my shirt. Another Scotsman intervened and ushered the drunk outside, recognizing me as he did so. When he returned he came across to me, held out his hand and in a broad Glaswegian accent apologized for intruding, saying, 'Scuse me, pal, hope you don't mind me being totally *stereotypical.*' I found that a wonderful turn of phrase, and it made my day.

Usually, it's small things like that which add a glow to the day – a passing remark, a shy request for an autograph from some ten-year-old kid. But there was one memorable encounter with some people a little higher up the social scale.

Lucy and I were at the Imperial War Museum, which had just been newly refurbished. It was quite an occasion. Royalty was present *en masse.* We were wandering round a war-weary Land Rover when there was the Queen, right in front of us. Quick as a flash, an aide introduced us, and she moved graciously on, leading a little crowd of notables. Then, as if they were just part of the crowd, Prince Andrew appeared, with the Duke of Edinburgh. Prince Andrew had served in the Falklands, and we had met at the Weston Spirit. 'I know this chap,' he said, and introduced us to the Duke, who asked about the injuries and my recuperation. I told him the story of how the Army doctors had grafted on undamaged skin taken from remote parts of my anatomy, ending with the news that a slice of backside had been used to rebuild my nose. 'So now, when a woman kisses me,' I finished, 'she doesn't know how close she is to kissing my bum.' It was an old joke, which Lucy had heard too often, but it must have been new to the Duke and the Prince, because they bellowed with laughter.

All this was brought into focus for me during my three years in Liverpool. I had needed to leave home for personal reasons –

I had gained a good deal of confidence, but needed to stand on my own feet at last. And after all she'd been through, my Mam needed *her* independence. After helping to establish the Weston Spirit, there seemed no reason for me not to stay on. I bought my first car – a low-slung, moonstone-blue Ford Sierra Cosworth, complete with tail-fin and spoiler, a great car for a fancy-free bachelor. I took out a mortgage and moved from lodgings to a little two-bedroomed semi in the suburb of Woolton, and set about making a new life.

But what did that mean? I still had no real idea. One thing I did know, was that I needed challenges, any sort of challenges. I liked being alive again, but I knew I couldn't expect to go through life wrapped in cotton wool. As the actor Anthony Quayle said, in his last television interview before he died, 'If you haven't got any danger in your life, hurry up and find some.'

One challenge that had already come my way was when I was offered the chance to learn to fly, financed by a Douglas Bader Scholarship under the control of the International Air Tattoo. It was a wonderful offer, and I'll always be indebted to the man who inspired the award.

As an ordinary soldier who had got injured, it's good to have extraordinary people to look up to, in particular disabled people who show through their lives how much can be achieved. Douglas Bader not only had guts, strength and competence, but he also knew how to use publicity to help people. It wasn't the fact of his injury that set him apart, but what he did with himself afterwards. He was the first double amputee to drive and fly, and certainly the first to go straight back into conflict. The late, great Douglas Bader was, is and always will be the man who, in my eyes, achieved the most for others as a result of being disabled. If I'm ever a quarter the man he was, then I shall feel I have achieved something in my life.

Anyway, I was just three hours away from qualifying for my pilot's licence when something happened that brought me up short. I was doing solo circuits around Liverpool airport in a strong wind. As I came in to land, the wind kept pushing me up and down, so that I had to keep changing my angle of descent. I was afraid that I would either overshoot or hit the ground with a bang, and decided to go around again. Next time the same thing happened. By now I was sweating buckets (that's one problem of being burned, by the way – it upsets the cooling mechanism). My imagination started to work overtime. If you come down wrongly, you come down hard, and there's little protection. The third time around I made it, and sat there with my heart racing, dripping sweat and muttering, 'No more.' Flying had not become an obsession with me and now I knew it never would. I didn't need that kind of risk-taking in my life.

But it did prepare me for a second challenge, which I might never have accepted if I hadn't done some flying. In the summer of 1989, someone organizing an air show at the US Air Force base at Fairford in Wiltshire called me up. He asked me if I would do something to raise money for the International Air Tattoo, the people who had given me the flying scholarship. I wanted to help. Besides, King Hussein of Jordan would be there. He sponsors six of the IAT scholarships, and I had met him once before, when I was learning to fly. All I had to do, according to the man, was some 'wing-walking'. It sounded pretty scary. He tried to reassure me: it didn't involve actually walking on a wing. I just had to stand there, tied on to the wing, upright.

I wasn't very reassured because I have a terrible fear of heights. As a kid, I had to be rescued off cliff-faces more than once. As soon as I look down, I'm finished. At a book-signing at Lloyds of London, I had to go along a glass walkway high above the main floor. There was nothing but glass between me and death. I fixed my eyes straight ahead and concentrated on putting one foot in front of the other. My fingers still tingle just thinking about that, not to mention my absolute major fear – parachuting.

13

Still, I do have this weakness: I will do almost anything for charity. If somebody were to offer me money for charity to jump out of an aeroplane with a parachute – mind you, it would have to be a *huge* amount, and I'd need a very big nappy – I'd do it.

So, of course, I said yes to the wing-walking. Well, I told myself, it can't be too risky – after all, the pilot will be wanting to get home to his wife and kids.

The day came. It was a sweltering summer's day and I arrived, with nerves twitching and sweating profusely.

It was a surprising experience. I found myself zipped into a windproof suit, immersed in a helmet and goggles, looking like Biggles, standing on the top of this high-performance biplane, strapped to a strut sticking up from the fuselage. We trundled out ready for take-off. The soft breeze swept away the summer heat, and all at once, I began to feel more secure. We took off. No panic, I suppose because there was nothing against which to measure our height. I even managed a few quick nervous little waves as we swept over the crowd.

It was coming into land that scared me. The plane seemed to crab-walk sideways towards the runway, and I'm sure the only reason we straightened up was because I was praying so hard. As we trundled to a halt I felt quite elated. I only realized what I'd been through when I stepped down. My knees were locked back, solid with tension. I felt as if I looked like Douglas Bader himself, clumping stiff-legged across the tarmac. Later, as promised, I met King Hussein. I'm sure he was as charming as ever, but I can't remember a word he said because he was with Queen Noor, who is an *extremely* attractive lady.

The next challenge was both more dangerous and more demanding. It started when I was on the TV show *Wogan*, when Terry asked me if there was any dream that I really wanted to fulfil. As it happened, I had always wanted to drive a fast car, ever since I was a kid, and I said so. I had my Sierra Cosworth, but I meant a *really* fast car, on a racing circuit. A few days later a PR company contacted me. Did I fancy trying my hand at racing to raise some money for the Weston Spirit?

My Mam and Gran were against the idea. 'What do you want to do something so bloody stupid for?' Gran had said, with her usual force. They were afraid of my getting burned again, especially as my real grandfather, Gran's first husband, had been mad keen on cars and had died in a motor cycle accident. But that didn't bother me much. I knew that racing drivers were well protected by fireproof suits and had no intention of refusing.

I found myself learning to race in a Ford XR3i on the Oulton Park circuit in Cheshire. I wasn't a natural by any means. My distorted hands were clumsy on the wheel and gear-lever. The first time around I could have been beaten by an ice-cream van. But I persevered, for two days a week, over a couple of months, getting to know the course and the machine, getting the feel of high-revving gear changes and learning to anticipate the critical moment when the back starts to slide as you go into a corner. It was a thrill, the double challenge of doing something so precise at such a high speed. Concentration and practice had their effect. At the end of the two months, I had knocked fifteen seconds off my lap time, and was within a second or two of my instructor's. I was ready for my first race.

It was October 1989. I was to drive a Sierra Cosworth in the Firestone Production Saloon Cars Race at Thruxton in Hampshire. I had my own Sierra Cosworth, of course, but this was different. The time leading up to the race was without a doubt the most nerve-racking of my life. I had really put myself on the line this time. Up in a plane, I was on my own; here, I would be in full view of both the public and the media, testing my new skills, challenging myself to overcome my disability, knowing that failure would set back the chances of other disabled people who wanted to race. The day before I could hardly eat. That night, I don't think I slept. When I arrived at the pit – far too early – I was like a new boy at school, with no idea what to say, where to put my clothes or when to change; all this, thirty-one other competitors, and twelve laps to go.

Well, I didn't disgrace myself. After an unnerving start – there was a crash on the first lap that put one driver in hospital – I managed to stay on the road, and came in twenty-fifth. It was enough to encourage me. I was no Nigel Mansell, but I knew I could improve.

Over the next year I competed in sixteen races, half a dozen of which I failed to finish. My disabilities didn't seem much of a hindrance after all, even though once my co-driver broke the gear-stick, leaving me to handle a jagged piece of metal that stripped the tender skin from my palm. I even managed to come in third on one occasion – not great, but not too bad for a beginner.

So in many ways things were going well. I was involved in charity work, and physical challenges had been overcome. But there was another sort of lack to be made up – nothing to do with my body, or me as a public figure, or achievement, but me as a person, the inner me.

Let me backtrack:

Immediately after the fire, I was terrified I'd never have a girlfriend again. I can joke about my looks now, but there was a time when every glimpse of myself in the mirror was enough to send shivers down me. I was frightened I looked so terrible that no one would ever look at me or touch me again. Time brought reassurance. In Liverpool I'd had a few girlfriends, and regained belief in myself as a man – but only to a certain degree.

I had developed a long-term, deep-seated urge to make a family, have children, put down roots, find stability. By the time I had started racing I knew that this, too, was at least a possibility.

A year before, in the summer of 1988, I was in the office when a girl walked in who I had never seen before. I couldn't help noticing her, because any man would. She had deep dark eyes like little pots of coal, and a gentle easy manner. There were only about half a dozen people in the office, and I knew all the others, so I naturally introduced myself. Her name was Lucy, and she was working part-time for Merseysports.

At that stage, neither of us gave the other much thought. I was just off to learn to fly; she was going to the United States to spend the summer working for Camp America. We parted as casual friends do – a little kiss on the cheek, a quick 'Look after yourself' – without any idea we would meet again. Even if I'd thought about it, I wouldn't have thought about it for long. I knew I was no humungous catch – scarred, bald, gammy hands, bit of a beer belly, and certainly no confidence I could get a pretty, spirited young girl to *marry* me.

In the autumn, when we were both back in Liverpool, we bumped into each other again at a Weston Spirit get-together. Soon after this she heard I had a terrible cold, and decided to see how I was.

It so happened that I had someone staying with me – Jane, a woman whose husband had died in the Falklands. I didn't know her well, but I'd invited her to stay, just to lay a few ghosts to rest. We were talking over a cup of tea when there was a knock on the door. It was Lucy.

She seemed embarrassed at finding Jane there. Suddenly, touched by her thoughtfulness, I realized that I wanted to see more of her. I had to do something, right then, to show her there was nothing going on between Jane and me, and yet not be rude to Jane. So I suggested we all go out for a Chinese meal. Luckily, after a little polite prevarication, Lucy agreed.

Then afterwards, just as she was going, I suggested she come with me and a couple of others to a football match – Newcastle United v. Manchester United – at St James's Park, Newcastle on Sunday, two days later.

It was a miserable day – rainy, windy and bitterly cold. We walked for ever from the car-park. During the match, a fight broke out behind us. I joked that Newcastle was often like this: you went for a fight, and sometimes, if you were lucky, a football match would break out right in front of you. That day, we were borderline lucky: it was a dead boring nil-nil draw. The only thing that lifted the day for me was that Lucy seemed happy to snuggle up to me. I fancied her something rotten.

That was really the start of it. Lucy seemed not only to like me – she liked football! It was obvious she would never *really* appreciate the finer points, because she was an Everton supporter. Being a Manchester United fan, of course, *I* could tell her what real football was all about. But if she could put up with rain, cold, aggro and a draw, she had to have something.

It didn't take long for me to realize what an extraordinary and wonderful person she was. Fortunately for me she wasn't bothered by my looks – mine or anybody else's, as far as I could see. It was a wonderful thing to be appreciated for myself rather than as 'the Falklands veteran' or the 'media personality'. She seemed always to look right through to the heart of people. As long as they were decent, she was nice to them. She didn't judge, and had no hatred for anyone except people who hurt children.

Soon I realized that knowing her was changing me. Like most men, I started off just being proud of her, with a 'look-at-this-girl-on-my-arm' attitude, as if I ought to be owning her. But I quickly realized I would never own Lucy, and that was one reason I had begun to fall in love with her.

After three months – in March 1989 – she moved in with me; and three months after that we got engaged. It was a funny time. The first book had just come out, and I didn't want any more publicity. On the other hand, once we knew we were going to get married, I wanted to mark the occasion. So one evening, when we went out for supper at an Italian restaurant with a couple of friends, I ordered a bunch of two dozen roses to be delivered. It took some elaborate planning, because I had bought the engagement ring – having managed to discover Lucy's size – and smuggled it along with me. Once there, I got the restaurant to hide the ring in the roses, then deliver them to Lucy while we were still eating. Of course throughout the meal I could hardly eat for nerves, but when the roses came, when she opened the note, when she saw the ring, when I saw her expression – just pure delight – I knew I had done the right thing.

Then, somehow, the press had got hold of it. All the newspapers wanted to take photographs. We refused. Reporters camped on the doorstep for several days. It was the first time that I appreciated how intrusive they could be. They seemed to assume they owned us. Lucy once had to walk straight past the house and on to the neighbours' for a cup of tea until they had gone. Two of them were really sleazy-looking guys from the tabloids, one with hair slicked back over the collar of his leather jacket, the other in a suit with tie skew-whiff, his collar undone and a note-pad in the pocket. *Stereotypical.* They were trying to get a story on Lucy and her ex-boyfriends, but she'd never really had any. There was no story, and eventually they went away.

So we managed to keep our privacy, up until the end of the year.

Around this time my professional life, such as it was, took another turn. Out of the blue, the BBC in Cardiff asked me to present a radio show entitled *Summer Gems*, which featured well-known Welshmen. I had to choose ten records and say what they meant to me.

I must have done something right, because two months later the BBC approached me again. Would I like to host my own show? Well who wouldn't? Soon, every Saturday, I had fifty minutes of music and a chat with a celebrity going out over South Wales and part of the Midlands. I enjoyed the work and loved having the chance to talk to people like Lenny Henry, Gary Glitter and Elkie Brooks about what interested them, and me, and (with luck) the listeners. The radio show was also the only bit of real routine I had in my life – something I was beginning to miss.

The only problem was, it meant driving 500 miles a week between Liverpool and Cardiff. It was expensive, and a strain, especially with the marriage getting closer.

This wasn't the only strain. I still haven't really forgiven Malcolm for what happened. My old and trusted friend, Malcolm Brinkworth, who had been largely responsible for the three documentaries, informed me that he was making a film about charities and wanted to include the Weston Spirit. Would I take a bunch of kids through an assault course up at Purbright?

Well, I would do almost anything for Weston Spirit and for Malcolm, so of course I agreed, never suspecting a thing. I cheered the kids over walls, along horizontal ladders and through rubber tyres, while the cameras rolled. Then, with the performance over, I was relaxing with the kids when I saw a strangely familiar figure approaching me.

It was Michael Aspel, and one of Malcolm's crew was a Thames TV cameraman, and This, out of the blue, Was My Life.

I was totally gobsmacked.

'You bastard!' I shouted at Malcolm. Trusted friend, indeed! He knew I hated surprises! 'You bastard, you lied to me!' Then I turned to Michael. I must have looked outraged, because he told me later he thought I was going to put one on his chin.

As it happened, despite my apprehension, everything was fine. We would have spoken to King Hussein directly from Jordan, if the satellite link hadn't broken down. And when Lucy came on, it was more than fine. This was the first time we really made a public statement of the engagement.

The next problem was the marriage. It occurred to me that it would be perfect if we could be married in the Guards Chapel, in London. It may seem strange these days for an ex-soldier to remain attached to his old regiment, but I certainly was, and still am. The chapel was the only place that seemed to hold any religious significance for me, because it spoke of things that will always be real to me – the boys I served with, especially those who died. Somehow, my old boss Brigadier Johnny Rickets heard of the engagement and my dream, and said he'd fix it.

We were married on 12 May 1990, the eighth anniversary of the day on which I sailed for the Falklands aboard the *QE2*, and almost twelve months after becoming engaged. My best man was Jimmy Salmon, who helped save my life on the *Sir Galahad*, and the service was conducted by the former Welsh Guards padre, Reverend Michael Walters. Lucy's chief bridesmaid, Susie Fowler, was a dream in a peach-coloured dress, and she had three other bridesmaids and my seven-year-old nephew Richard as a page-boy.

Everything was perfect – the service, the band, the wine, the food – except that nerves turned the whole thing into a nightmare for me. I'm still not too certain about some of the details. If there hadn't have been a video and so many pictures it would all have remained a blur.

I remember getting changed in the sergeants' mess and then nipping downstairs with Jimmy for an ale – anything to take my mind off what was going to happen. Then there we were the two of us, Jimmy in his red Welsh Guards tunic wearing his Northern Ireland and Falklands medals, me in morning dress, being greeted by friends and relatives.

Already there was a crowd outside the railings. I was thankful that the security was good. Even so, two respectable old ladies who had come up from Brighton specially for the occasion had managed to slip past into the chapel, uninvited. No one minded, and they have provided us with a few laughs since, seeing them on the video tiptoeing here and there, trying to avoid the camera.

I remember standing, shifting my feet in an agony of apprehension, staring up at the golden mosaics behind the altar – the chapel was bombed in the war, and this was the only surviving bit of the original. I remember staring at my fingers – one of them was plastered, because I had somehow managed to cut myself that morning. I remember wondering: did I take the price off the bottom of my shoes, for when I kneel down? I remember the Trumpet Voluntary and Lucy appearing beside me. I had been told not to look at her, but I couldn't resist a sly peak. She looked a dream in great swathes of ivory.

Then a little bit of drama. We were well on our way, with the Rev. Mike doing his stuff, and me wiping the sweat from my forehead, trying to concentrate on Mike's words of wisdom. He was giving us a talk about marriage having its downs as well as its ups, and had just mentioned 'the pressures that cause us to stumble', when, as if on cue, *whump*! there was a heavy thud from behind.

We turned, and there was Susie out for the count. She'd fainted, poor girl, right on Lucy's train. Wondering what was going to happen, I looked anxiously at Mike. He could see that Jimmy was already helping her up and that she would be all right. 'Don't worry,' he whispered, 'the funeral service is on the next page.'

A few minutes later, with Susie back in action, we were on our way out, down the banner-hung nave, with the band playing the Pomp and Circumstance march. We posed briefly for an army of photographers, and led off into the hall nearby for a sit-down meal.

It was magnificent, I know it was. I just wish I could remember it. But I had a speech to make, and I knew I was going to be terrible, and I was terrible, and the whole experience was too wonderful and too nerve-racking for me to take it in.

So it was a bit of a relief to return to motor racing. Not for long, though.

It was almost the end of the season at Oulton Park in October 1990. It had been raining, and the surface was still slick. I was coming off a bend called Druids, at over ninety m.p.h., swinging a bit wide. I put two wheels on the grass, and then turned a little too sharply to regain the road. The car skidded, spun sideways, and hit a retaining wall of Armco, which smashed the back end off. I ended up 300 metres down the road. I don't remember the crash itself. I must have blacked out. I honestly believe that if you die in a crash, you know nothing at all about it.

I came to, hearing one of the marshals telling me, 'Stay where you are.'

'You've got to be joking!' I yelled, in less polite terms, because there was one thought in my head – fire! – and I threw myself out in a forward roll away from the car. I sat on the Armco and took off my helmet, mildly shocked and so embarrassed I hardly registered the bruised ribs and aching, whiplashed neck.

That ended the season, and, for all I know, my short racing career. There was no sponsorship for the following season, and I couldn't say I was sorry. I had enjoyed racing. It was nothing to do with being attracted to danger. It is far safer than people think, and no more dangerous, statistically, than rock-climbing, hang-gliding or microlighting. But I'd done enough to know that it wasn't going to be a career. It demanded total commitment to the machine, to technique, to the team behind you. Hours, days, weeks, years of concentration. That's what it takes to be a winner, not just talent. Even if I had had the talent, I knew I would never have been able to commit myself to the life.

Anyway, I had a new and better life now. Lucy and I had settled into marriage. We might have been in Liverpool still if it hadn't been for that weekly journey to Cardiff – that, combined with a puzzling, worrying sequence of not-so-petty crimes.

Although I didn't know it at the time, the trouble had started one day when I was in the office. Someone had come in and said they'd seen a youth tampering with my much-loved Sierra

Cosworth. I ran out but was too late to catch the culprit. He had used a screwdriver to break a door-lock and one of the alarms, but had failed to get in. There was no reason to think there was anything sinister going on – the car was a highly prized item worth stealing. I just put it down to bad luck.

But over the next few months, there were four more attacks – another on the Cosworth and three on two other sponsored cars – both 4 × 4 Sierras – one of which was actually stolen, and subsequently recovered after a police chase. In all, there was several thousand pounds' worth of damage. OK, they weren't my cars, but I had to pay the insurance on them, and I began to wonder if it was the cars themselves they were after, or what they thought might be *in* the cars? And why would they think there might be something in them worth stealing? Did they know they were my cars? Was this personal?

The thing that really set me worrying was when they had a go at Lucy's 1.4 Orion (my Sierra was in the garage). It was the cheapest out of sixteen cars on the street. There was a 1600 injection Orion in front of us, a brand new 1800 Sierra behind us, and further down the street stood a Lotus and a brand new XR21 among others, all much more powerful than Lucy's Orion, which contained nothing more than a cheap radio-cassette player. And it didn't only happen once. There were three attempted break-ins in three weeks. The house was an ordinary little two-bedroom semi, but I was beginning to wonder: if this is personal, how soon before they get inside the house?

So we decided to move south, back to the valleys, back to my roots. We chose a plot of land on a new estate, on a hilltop high above a hamlet, even before the foundations had been put down, and moved in October 1990. My home village, Nelson, was only a mile away. I felt a renewed sense of belonging, being cradled again by crags and ridges and grassed-over tips, while over the hill were the familiar lines of terraced houses I remembered so well from my childhood.

Practically, as well, it made a lot of sense. Lucy now had neighbours to talk to, and we were closer to some of my oldest friends. Mam and Gran were nearby. Mam is a district nurse, which was a great help when James was on the way.

Then along came James, and a new meaning to life, and deeper questions about my past, present and future.

One thing I was sure of: charity work was something I would always do, if I had the opportunity. I enjoy fund-raising for charities. I enjoy the challenge, the satisfaction of working with people, and for people, and the exhilaration of reaching a target. It really gives me a high, an uplifting burst of feeling in my stomach, as if I were a child again, suddenly discovering I've done something well.

There is one group of people I feel great empathy for: burns victims. Being burned myself taught me how easily you accept humiliation, how much you want to hide, and how important it is to show yourself. Only by making that statement can you accept yourself as you are, and make other people accept you. That's one of many reasons I'm grateful to Malcolm – the documentaries showed a burned person beginning to live a normal life. It really made a difference to the way the public perceived injuries that had just been ignored before. Now people often say to victims who are recovering after being caught in fires, 'Oh you've been burned – like Simon Weston.' By providing a point of reference, that helps both sides – the scarred and the healthy – to accept the wounds and the problems. That's one development I would never have predicted, and one thing that makes some sense of my injuries.

It's not just burns victims, though. As a burns victim I'm also one of a larger minority, the disabled. Because I know the good it can do, I'm always ready to take up a challenge on their behalf. They should know it's OK to fight, and that standing up for a cause can bring results. People shouldn't take it for granted that someone else is responsible. 'It doesn't affect me; I'm nineteen; I can drink fifteen pints of lager; I'm great and stuff the world' – this was me, once, and look what happened. So many go through life without even *thinking* about disabled people – yes, they exist, but they belong somewhere else, to somebody else, in a home. But take a group of people in any pub – out of every hundred, there are two or three who are registered with some form of disability. They should be seen with more than a sympathetic glance. People should say, 'That is me, or a friend, or a relative, in a few years' time.' They should realize that everything they do now for others could help them or their relatives eventually.

So often now I see issues, small and big, that need action. Take disabled parking. Often people who are themselves not disabled but who have a disabled partner or relative display the disabled person's car sticker, even when they don't have the person with them, because this way they can park the car more easily. But it's not right. They ought to get fined for doing it. The law ought to be tougher. I believe it's something to fight for, or at least *part of* something to fight for.

That's why I was so pleased to be given the opportunity to get involved with the Royal Star and Garter Home, the organization that looks after disabled and injured ex-servicemen and women. They've been in existence seventy-six years now, and they need cash to refurbish their main building in London. I was happy to help. It's a wonderful cause – two world wars and over seventy smaller conflicts have involved hundreds of thousands of men and women who never know when they might need help. One day – who knows – I might be one of them.

The place is full of amazing and deserving characters, like the man who woke up to find he had a form of multiple sclerosis. It took him seven years in the Royal Star and Garter Home to learn to walk again. Then there was Owen, who had been captured by the Nazis, been force-marched through snow, contracted frostbite, and had both feet amputated by the Red Cross. Another old bloke, Horace Ham, is ninety-five. He was wounded on the first day of the Battle of the Somme in the First World War, and returned to the front to do twelve 'over-the-tops'. After the war, for the next seventy years, he was fine. Then, without any family left, he needed someone to provide him with some care. There he was, with a room of his own, still able to keep his independence and to enjoy his game of snooker.

But however rewarding charity work is, it isn't enough to build a whole life on. I had no professional direction. Challenges had been met; but they were not enough. There were causes to fight for; but I wasn't sure what my role could be. I wasn't sure I could raise cash, hire and fire, get sponsors, do all the things that professional charity-workers do. I felt restless and unfocused. Becoming a father had forced me to think about all this, and the future. If I couldn't work out my own destiny, what hope had I of helping others? Of guiding James?

And it wasn't just a lack of professional direction. The truth was there were hidden fears gnawing at me, fears I had no idea how to face, but that had to be faced sometime. I knew I would never be able to move forward, to build on whatever I had achieved, for myself, for others, for Lucy, for James, unless I faced them.

I had never imagined the road to recovery would be so long, or that it would ever lead me back to a wind-whipped shore eight and a half thousand miles away.

But the time had come.

I had to go back to the Falklands.

2

THE REASONS WHY

October 1991

There was nothing new about the idea of going back. I had first expressed a wish to return to Malcolm, not long after the war.

I could have gone years earlier. I had received half a dozen offers to go back; they were there almost from the word go. But at that time I would only have considered returning with the boys, with a big bunch of Welsh Guards, so that we could honour the lads in the best way possible – partying all the way there and all the way back. That's how they would have mourned us, and that's how they would like to be mourned – with a lot of alcohol, a lot of laughter, a lot of sarcasm. It's the soldier's way of dealing with impossible emotions.

Once a friend was kind enough to fix up the flights for me, on my own. Mam asked me what I'd do if I went. I said I wanted to go to San Carlos, where I had first landed, to the huge freezer plant, used as a hospital, where I almost died, and to the shore where they put the boys to rest. I said I'd like to walk the final few hilly miles over Mount Longdon, Tumbledown, Wireless Ridge – the places that had given their names to battles, and become household names in 1982 – to

Port Stanley, because I had never made it all the way the first time.

'Take some daffodils,' Mam said, because it was spring when we had this conversation. 'Throw some daffodils in the water.'

'I wouldn't do that, Mam,' I said. 'The boys would rather have cans of beer.'

In the end, even though I had the chance, I didn't want to know. It wasn't right for me then. In fact, it was so far from what I wanted that I forgot the whole conversation. It's only Mam who remembers.

Somewhere along the way, though, I began to change. Gradually, almost without realizing, I found I needed a different way of coping, something more personal, something deeper: a return.

But not *just* a return. Malcolm and I agreed that it would make a subject for a fourth film – the last one, definitely the last – but we both knew for different reasons that there had to be something more.

I already knew what that 'something more' had to be. A strange idea had resurfaced, one that had been with me for years. It was this: that one day, somehow, I would meet the pilot who had dropped the bomb on the *Sir Galahad*.

I never took the possibility seriously, until talking to Malcolm brought it sharply into focus. With his involvement in the making of the documentary, I might be able to achieve my ambition.

By 1991 it had become a reality. Malcolm knew the pilot's name – although to me it didn't yet mean enough to stick in my mind – and believed that the meeting could be arranged. For him, as a film director, the time was right. The tenth anniversary of the war was approaching. For me, the time was not perfect, not with James so small and growing so fast. But I knew there never would be a perfect time. I made my decision: better now than never, better face what had to be faced, if the rest of my life was to make any sense.

Backed by the BBC, plans hardened; we were to set off in early November.

I was so wound up it was hard to believe. I would sit in my chair, holding James and wondering about things that my teenage self would have thought totally weird. Where was my life going? Why this urge to return to the scene of destruction, death and horror? What good would it do me – or anyone else?

You might say it would have been better to leave well alone. The same thought occurred to me, many times, with increasing force.

In October, there was a commemoration ceremony for three of the lads who died – Cliff Ellie, Brian Jasper and Ian Anthony Dale – all in my platoon, and all from the same school, Hawthorn High in Pontypridd. I didn't know them well, but each had a memory attached to him. I used to play rugby with Cliff. After the bomb struck, he ran back into the inferno to do what he could to help, and never came out. Brian had left the Army once, and had recently rejoined. He had had two little girls, I remember. Ian had slept next to me on the way down on the QE2. I remember him telling me that his wife was pregnant.

It was a moving service, with a couple of hymns and the unveiling of simple plaques in the foyer. As I looked across at the families, as I talked to them afterwards, I began to feel more and more like a traitor. I was less than a month away from meeting the man who had caused the death of their sons. Was I really doing the right thing by going back? I didn't want to offend any of the friends or relatives. They, and hundreds of others, remember every single day that sons, fathers, husbands, cousins, uncles, friends will never return. I didn't want to make those memories more painful than they already were. Nor did I want them to think I was being disloyal to the dead. Certainly, I didn't want anyone to think I was forgiving the pilot on their behalf.

But my intentions wouldn't be enough. I came away believing as firmly as I have ever believed anything that, if I went, if I met the pilot, if I treated him like another human being, I risked losing the respect of many people both in military and in civilian life, especially those who had lost friends or relatives.

Did this mean I shouldn't go? As I thought about it, I realized that I could not be responsible for the way other people reacted. I would simply have to take whatever came at me, and try to make people see that this was something I had to do for myself, however hard it would be, and whatever the risks, because otherwise I wouldn't be able to live my life to the full, and then I'd be no use to anyone.

If there would be anything to forgive, I hoped I would be forgiven. If I managed to find anything positive in the experience, I hoped that I would be able to pass it on.

Why was I going back? It was a question I asked myself every day now.

I didn't particularly *want* to go back. There wasn't a lot there to see. It wasn't as if I was about to bind myself permanently to that place and that time, like an old soldier from the First World War returning to the Somme. A glimpse of bare hills and a forty-five minute shopping spree in Port Stanley, and that would be it, right?

It's simply that I *had* to go back, just this once. There was something in me that *needed* to go back. There was something missing, some lack, something to be completed. But what?

I had thought and thought about this. And I didn't know. I wished I did, but I didn't. All I knew was there was a feeling of emptiness. There were times when I thought, 'I'm throwing my life away, because I'm not achieving enough.' Then I went through a phase when I was working non-stop for about six or eight weeks without a day off. I was here, there, a school to visit, a launch, an opening, a speech. I couldn't wait for a rest. Then I got my rest and I thought, 'I'm wasting my life away again.' I was never satisfied – fed up with doing too much, and fed up with not doing enough.

Restlessness and confusion. Same as many people my age. But why should feeling restless and confused have made me want – no, *need* – to go back? It seemed to be time to look deeper.

Perhaps I had to experience something I never properly experienced at the time. I was never a part of the war. I didn't even hear any guns fired. The closest I got to action, before the bomb struck, was when I was on the *Fearless* and saw two Sea Darts zip up towards two Argentinian Canberra bombers. One plane blew up. That was it. The sum total of my experience of action, until I was just about to go ashore at Fitzroy.

I never even saw much of the spot where I was injured. A quick peek above deck, a glimpse of treeless hills, a shiver in the gusty wind, and I was back below, in pursuit of warmth and a cup of tea. I was never a part of the injury process, because it was over so quickly. I heard the air-raid warning, squatted down, and then it was boom, whoosh, and I was out of it. It must have taken no more than twenty minutes, perhaps half an hour, to get me off. It was so quick I never really had a chance to understand, to assimilate.

Perhaps there was unfinished grieving – for myself, and for my friends.

There was reason enough for grief. I had been injured. I had lost my friends. I had lost my youth. I had lost my middle twenties. I had lost my job. I had lost my sport. I had lost what might have been, what I might have become – my future. Having come out the other side obviously I've gained in certain aspects, but the losses – I still feel them tremendously. They don't go away.

But the sense of loss was disturbing. It lacked a focus. I'm not an angry person, so I didn't blame anyone for what had happened. Right from the beginning my Mam worked at building on only positive feelings in me. I had no one to blame but myself, she said. It was my decision to join up. People get hurt in war. It was no good moaning – I had to take responsibility for my own fate. I wondered: was it not having someone to blame that made me feel this strange, unfocused restlessness?

Certainly, perhaps most of all, I still missed the boys who had died. I had joined up with some of them. Some of them had come to my house. I remember once, just before we left for the Falklands, arriving home in a one-ton vehicle with three other lads. One of them, Gareth Hughes, was a Welsh Guard (the other two were REME – Royal Electrical and Mechanical Engineers – blokes). Gareth was the driver. We were on our way back from Cardiff to our base in Brecon Beacons, and were eager for some home cooking. 'Seems like more boys here than there are in the whole Army!' Mam had said, and whipped up masses of egg, corned beef, chips, and apple tart. We ate her out of house and home, then roared off, more worried about running out of diesel than about leaving my Mam destitute and starving.

Now all I've got is the memory. I never had a chance to say goodbye. Saying goodbye is part of grieving. You need that sense of occasion, a little bit of time to realize your loss – something spiritual, if you like, though I am not a religious person at all.

The first time I really began to understand what had happened was when my Mam came to see me in hospital with a list of those who had died. She'd been to the memorial service. On the service-sheet were the names of everyone who had died. When she saw me, she laid it on the line, reading the list, with me crying like a kid from beneath my newly made eyelids. She was afraid that if she didn't confront me, I would never take it on board, never be able to grieve, never come to terms with the loss.

Perhaps that hadn't been enough.

The grief came through in odd little thoughts. My penknife, wallet and poker dice were all lying on the sea-bed in Port Pleasant. My rifle – that must still be aboard the *Galahad*. My pack. My book – I was making my way through a paperback, *The Legionnaire*. Small things that represented a huge part of my life. The *Galahad* is a war-grave now – she was sunk two miles out to sea – but it might help to see the spot where she was hit.

I thought I'd been through the whole grieving process. You'd think nine years would be long enough.

But perhaps the grieving couldn't be complete until I'd come full circle.

Perhaps I also needed to reassess the whole experience of the war in some more objective way.

Strangely, I couldn't feel bitter about what had happened. It would be easy if we could sit around pointing the finger and blaming. But in war, sacrifices are made, lives are lost, things are asked of normally placid, decent men that would never be asked of them at other times. This is true on both sides.

When I thought of the Argentinians, I didn't think 'enemy'. I know there are people and armies who love the power and authority they've been given, or they've taken. The Khmer Rouge and the East German Stasi, for example, both seemed to enjoy destroying people's lives. But I didn't feel it was like that with the Argentinian armed forces. I thought they were misled. The media were state-owned, and those in power could tell people what they liked; there weren't many dissidents to counter them. The war we fought was the creation of one man and his government trying to alleviate their problems. It looked easy: thirty marines, 1,800 people, a few windswept hills. They never thought Britain would send an army 8,500 miles to protect a few sheep farms. A major mistake. I couldn't hold anybody, except a few of the leaders, responsible for being caught up in an error they had no control over.

Fine, I could understand the Argentinians being a bit aggrieved – they started it, and we finished it. That's war. There's got to be a winner and there's got to be a loser. Of course, in a way, everybody's a loser in war. But in limited, military terms there has to be seen to be a victor. Luckily – and there was a lot of luck involved – it was a conventional conflict, solved conventionally, by the seizure of arms, equipment, and men. We won, they lost.

And I was still convinced it was a just war, if any war is just. I hate, loathe and detest warfare, yet I was not ashamed to say I was a soldier who loved the Army, and that I had fought in a conflict I believed to be right. Most of my mates felt the same.

Once you're in a situation of war, there's nothing else you can do about it. You can't afford to think about the arguments for and against. You have to go there and do your job, otherwise you're dead. You don't want to take life, but if you have to, you will. There was an aggressor who needed to be stopped, in the only way possible – open conflict. Politics were beside the point. We did what we did because at the time it was the right thing to do.

None of us wanted to be there. None of us even knew where Argentina or the Falklands were. None of us was really interested in Argentina, apart from the fact that it had a football team, and that the Argentinians weren't too bad at polo and hockey. Other than this nobody knew a great deal about them, and not too many of us cared.

But when you sign up for the armed forces, you sign on a dotted line. In between each dot is an unwritten rule: you're signing up to kill or be killed, to maim or be maimed.

It's a tragedy of life that armed forces are necessary. But they'll remain necessary until all political disputes are settled and all terrorists content. Until then, mothers' sons will die.

By the time this book comes out, a lot more mothers' sons will have died. Whether they be Catholic or Protestant, British or Argentinian, Israeli or Arab, Croat or Serb, every soldier is some mother's son, and he deserves to live.

That's how I felt about the Argentinians. I felt sorry for the way they were lied to and the way that they were forced into war – how could anyone force a teenager to go to war? On the *Canberra*, there were five captured Argentinians, the youngest of whom (we were told) was just thirteen. I was on board ship with wounded kids of seventeen and under. Tragic.

But life is not a cute business in which we can all go around patting each other's faces with buttercups. The hard truth is that a teenager with a machine-gun can be as deadly as a marine. If he's wearing the opposition's uniform, and he's got a gun in his hand, you have to assume that he's prepared to kill you. That's where kill or be killed comes in. It's you or him.

With hindsight, you can say things should have been different. The politicians should never have allowed the conflict to escalate. But, as I saw it, there was no point feeling bitter even about the politics of the war. Neither at the time nor afterwards did I believe that political cynicism influenced our government's decision to go to war; it was not making a deliberate attempt to win an election by its action. Of course, the Conservatives awarded themselves Brownie points after the event. But one thing about Mrs Thatcher – she is a mother. She turned out the Air Force to find her son when he was lost in the desert. She took a lot of flak for doing so, but she did only what any mother would have done, given the power. I couldn't see her callously sending off a load of mothers' sons to battle, just to win an election.

This is what came to me when I tried to assess the war objectively. But perhaps it would all change when I went back.

Perhaps I needed to go just to meet the man who had done this to me, the pilot who had dropped the bomb. Maybe it sounds perverse, this urge to meet the man who had killed my friends, who had burned my old life away together with half my skin, but I wanted to talk to him, to find out how he felt about it, to look into his eyes, to see if there was a soul in there.

Now I had the chance, and I was scared of what I would feel when I met him. But it also challenged me, and offered the opportunity of some form of release that I couldn't understand.

Why scared? I didn't know. I didn't resent or hate him. I suppose I should have hated him. He had taken away my friends. I tried to find reasons why I should, but I couldn't, and I was sure I wouldn't unless he turned out to be a hateful personality. I was not going to dislike him just because he was doing his job, doing what a serviceman does in a battle. And there was nothing to forgive, because there was nothing to blame him for. If I'd had the chance to do it to him, I probably would have. How could I hate him for doing something that in ordinary circumstances he would never have done to me? But the circumstances were extraordinary, and he was carrying out his orders, doing his duty; you can't blame a man for that, even if it means killing forty or fifty men.

Sometimes I wondered if he was like me at all. Quite possibly that pilot had not lifted a finger in anger since. Perhaps, like me, he was more than happy to live peacefully. Perhaps, like me, he had found it a wonderful thing to say 'Good morning', 'Hello', 'How are you?' After being in action, there's a daily joy in the simple assertion that you're at peace with the world. Most people take such things for granted, like driving the same route to work every day for twenty years. Not me. I was still delighted just to be alive. Perhaps the pilot felt like this, too.

Or perhaps not. Perhaps this guy with a background so different from mine was an arrogant sod proud of his kills, some vindictive lout who went around crowing about the number of Welsh Guards he had taken out, someone I would be happy to part from his teeth. If I imagined him to be like that, yes, I could feel anger stirring. Then I hoped he would be like that, because it would be good to have a go, to take revenge for myself and my mates.

But it didn't last. My mood would change, and next time I would think: perhaps he was a slum kid, making good in the Air Force, the pride of his parents; or from some cowboy ranching family on the pampas; or maybe he was from Patagonia, from one of those pioneering sheep-breeding families who had moved from Wales a century ago. Maybe we had ancestors in common. Now there was a strange thought.

Anyway, he must be intelligent, tough, expert, to make a pilot. Was he married? Did he have kids? What was he feeling when he took off that day? Two very different people, linked by a brutal destiny, our lifelines suddenly snapping together. We were bound, and divided, by a terrible event. He had been only a few feet from me as the bomb flashed past me. At what point did our fates interlock? When did the damage he did to me and my mates become 'inevitable'? From the minute he climbed into the cockpit? From the minute he was born?

So back and forth went my thoughts – now calm, now with a twist of anger – though I knew that was only my imagination at work. But always there was an edge of fear to the thought of meeting him.

And when the tension built, I thought: well, after all, there's nothing extraordinary in what I'm about to do. Similar things have happened countless times, in countless wars. It gave me solace about meeting this guy, that English and German officers, fairly soon after the war, had felt more linked by the experience imposed on them than divided by their old enmity. British and U-boat sailors, British and German pilots – they couldn't forget, but they could forgive. The strange thing was, when they met, they found that there was nothing, in the end, to forgive.

It sounded easy when I said it. The trouble was, it didn't reassure me. I was still scared, scared that it was all a bit too easy. I felt like a kid whistling in the dark to keep away the bogey-men, to keep away the thought that when I met him, he would turn out not to be simply a pilot, but a tormentor, a sadist, a torturer. Then the fear would return, fear that emotions I could only guess at would leap up at me from the darkness, and no amount of whistling could keep the fear away.

Perhaps in returning I was looking for some way to cope with emotions about my survival. I often wondered why I hadn't died in the fire. Why me, and not the others? Could I have done more to save them?

Perhaps I'm a born survivor. Perhaps my unconscious had told me that if I were going to die, I'd better make sure I died in Wales. Perhaps, as my mother says, I just hated the idea of dying in water. Perhaps I came back just to annoy my mother and to spite my mate Carl, who'd get the 400 LPs I'd promised him if I didn't make it. But joking about it didn't help make sense of anything, and sense is what I needed.

When I remembered the few seconds immediately before and after the bomb struck – not that I did so often those days – I could see myself heading for my mate, Yorkie, who was fast asleep. I was going to shout in his ear, slap him on the back of the head, and wake him up. Lazy sod, why should he be asleep when I was awake?

Now, because I was running towards Yorkie, when everyone else was concentrating on getting ready to go ashore, perhaps that was the tiny injection of aggression I needed to do what I did. I remember the intercom squawking 'Air raid!', me squatting down in self-protection, the extraordinary grey streak of the bomb as it whipped through the ship before my eyes, the sudden rainbow flare of the explosion, the burst of flame, the moving fireballs of my mates, the choking smoke, swollen heads, blackened flesh, burning clothes, my own hands beginning to melt as I watched, the man I tried to help, falling through my hands, slippery as a roasting chicken, my skin flaking off on his uniform, uselessly, and then the terrible sprint through smoke and flames to the fresh air. I would have died if I'd stayed to help him. But I still have nine fingers, and he's dead.

Could I have done more and still lived? Might I have saved lives, even if it meant losing my own? I was with mates, and I knew their lives depended on me, and mine on them, and yet, when the moment came, I had failed them.

Those few seconds, when I ran – was I driven by self-preservation, or cowardice? Perhaps I did what I could. Perhaps nothing would have made any difference. But the fact of my survival made me doubt, and from the doubt sprang guilt, and the guilt was still with me. It will be with me for ever.

The only way I could cope was to make sure that I lived my life for a purpose.

So my feeling of emptiness had to have something to do with my future. There's a lot that I'd like to do. I'd like to win at something sporting, to own nice things, to earn well, do college courses, travel, do well on the radio – not that I'm a Steve Wright or a Simon Bates or a Dave Lee Travis, not a pushy, drive-hard-till-you-drop sort of person. But I needed to do *something*. I'd like to be free to discover what, and this trip was about achieving that freedom.

This in its turn had something to do with being in the public eye. This part of my life bothered me; it didn't seem real to me. I don't think of myself as being well known. I don't like being told I'm famous. I don't keep mementoes. I don't read much about myself. I never watch anything about myself on TV. At heart, I don't think I'm that media-worthy. I may do something that catches the imagination of the press now and then, but apart from this, I think I lead far too boring a life for them. This is what I wanted – an ordinary family life.

One thing was for sure – it had been a very strange experience, being me over the last ten years. All this talking and writing, especially as it was all about someone so young, and someone who had done so little. There's nothing unique or clever about being burned, or about my recovery. What was I going to do – *not* recover? It was as if I was two people: the public me – the way I had lived my life since my injuries, the way I had coped with my injuries – and the private me; but yet not two people, because the private me *was* the public me. I had just carried on doing what I enjoyed doing and what I thought was right; it wasn't worth all the attention. I was fairly certain the general public would one day have had enough of Simon Weston.

This isn't to say I knocked the publicity. I hated to think that all that experience might come to nothing. I wanted to be able to put it to good effect. But how?

I felt my life was an alphabet, with bits of the beginning and lots of gaps. If I looked hard between A and C I might find B. Then I'd have to find other letters, and then see if I could spell anything. I never was much of a speller, so I worried. What did I do today? Was it right? Was it useful and meaningful? Or did I just waste today, throw twenty-four hours away? All I knew was that somewhere along the line achievement was really important. I just wished I knew what it was I was supposed to achieve. If I didn't go crazy, maybe I would find some answers.

Later, with a little bit of luck, perhaps I would be able to transfer some of that understanding to my son. I would love him to understand the things that have baffled me, see some of the things I've seen, learn some of the things I've learned, know some of the people I've known. I hoped and prayed this was to be a journey that would benefit the two of us.

And ultimately I had to come away from the Falklands laughing. Whatever else I felt, if I didn't come away laughing as well it would haunt me for the rest of my life. There would be a few tears when I got there – bound to be – but unless I came away with some laughter there would be something left undone.

There was only one thing for it: to go.

3

BUENOS AIRES

15 November 1991

It was going to be a demanding trip, to say the least.

For me, it was a direct challenge, and I had no idea how I would take it all: meeting people we had been at war with; travelling, with all the tensions that involves; new places; new food; new beer (now that could be a real worry); and, most significantly, the strain of meeting the pilot and going back to the scene of my injury.

But I would also be part of a process – the making of a documentary. This involved a dozen people, a lot of money, a lot of preparation, and a lot of pressure – on me, and on the others, particularly Malcolm. We would be going with a television crew: a cameraman, an assistant cameraman, a sound man, an assistant producer and a production manager. This would be the first time a documentary about the war had involved both British and Argentinians. If the logistics were tough, the political arrangements were horrendous. The little I heard of them made me amazed that anything had been successfully organized at all.

Then there were the others: my co-writer, and a journalist from the *News of the World*, which had bought the serial rights and was eager to keep an eye on its investment; and, later, in the Falklands, a photographer was to join us.

Finally, there were the two Falklands veterans, who were vital both to the film and to me. I knew their support would be important, and I was sure I would benefit from a good dose of cynical Army humour. Their presence added a whole other dimension to the arrangements, because one of them was still serving. There had been little, if any, contact between Argentinian armed forces and our lads.

My own personal journey, the film, the book, the squaddies, the travel, the politics – the overlapping interests involved meant conflicting pressures for everyone. What could possibly go wrong? Practically anything – and everything.

It had always been important for me, and for the film, to take other military people with us. At first, I had wanted to make the trip with some other Welsh Guards. That had seemed right – Welsh Guards honouring other Welsh Guards. But very few of the Welsh Guards had been involved in fighting. Like me, they had had a limited war. It was important for the documentary that my companions should have wider experiences than mine, not identical ones.

But they couldn't be too different. I had no interest in going down there with pilots or sailors or SAS men. They would have to be from the regular Army, so that their experiences would balance mine, as well as extend it. And they had to be squaddies, not officers, so that they could convey the feel of war at its most basic. We could take no more than two or three men.

In the end, Malcolm had chosen two: Gary Tytler, then a lance-corporal, now a colour-sergeant from the 2nd Battalion, Scots Guards, and John Meredith, a platoon sergeant, later a warrant officer, with the 2nd Battalion, Parachute Regiment, usually referred to simply as '2 Para'. Both had seen the war through to the end, in vicious hand-to-hand fighting, in freezing, wet and windy misery.

I knew we would get on, right from the first meeting in the pub at the bottom of my hill. We talked about mutual friends. The Army is a small world, and we all knew both Welsh Guards and Scots Guards, who train in the same depot. John remembered many of them from a drill course at the depot, and he had also been an instructor at Brecon, where the Guards do their NCO training. I knew some Territorial paratroopers that John knew, because Paul Oginsky, co-founder of the Weston Spirit, was also a TA paratrooper.

That first meeting was a bit strained, because there was some filming going on as well, but it was enough for me to see they were both great lads, and supreme professionals. We bounced off each other and shared the same sense of humour, though they were both very different from me and from each other.

Gary was lean and fit, with a steely gaze and a trim moustache, the image of the fighting man. He had joined up at fifteen, left later for five years, then rejoined. He was quietly spoken, with a brilliant turn of phrase, but there was a menace to his quietness and humour. God help anyone who came up against him. He had fought virtually the length of Tumbledown on the bitter night of 13/14 June, and had been mentioned in dispatches for showing qualities of leadership at a crucial stage. He had fighting stories to make your hair stand on end, and to make you disgrace yourself with laughter, sometimes both at once.

John seemed a very different type. He had the army in his blood. His father had been in the Royal Welsh Fusiliers and the Paras, so John knew what the life meant long before he joined up at seventeen. He had served for over twenty years. Now around forty, he had left the Army just over a year before and had put on a bit of weight. At first sight, he gave the impression of a jovial father-figure. There was nothing jovial about his looks ten years earlier, but there was something to the father-figure image – his job had been to make sure his men were working as a team. He had to know not just how to drive them, but how to encourage them and how to protect them. He also had to fight with them. While Gary was helping to seize Tumbledown, John and his sixteen men had helped to take Wireless Ridge, a couple of miles away.

Like me, they were to meet Argentinians who would be as far as possible their opposite numbers, men who had tried to defend Tumbledown and Wireless Ridge. I had quite enough to worry about with the planned meeting with the pilot, and wasn't so interested in these other guys. But Gary and John were looking forward to meeting them, if only to ask a few professional questions. They didn't have the same sense of apprehension as me. After all, they hadn't been wounded, didn't have my emotional burdens, and didn't have to worry so much about a public image.

Well, so they thought. They were both so direct and so vivid in the way they talked that I was fairly sure they would have a public image after the documentary, even though they had none before.

16–20 November 1991

Buenos Aires turned out to be a major surprise. I didn't know what to expect, nor did Gary or John, but we certainly expected some sort of reaction to the presence of British servicemen among former enemies. And my image of the city was of a ramshackle, filthy South American capital, labouring under an oppressive government, where people were starving because of explosive inflation.

One first impression confirmed part of my image. As we drove in from the airport, a roadside sign stated: 'The Malvinas are Argentinian!' So apparently the political issues behind the war had not changed. Perhaps we really were among enemies.

Later, a glance at a map confirmed what the sign claimed: there were the Falklands, coloured a soft pink, labelled 'Islas Malvinas'. The capital, in huge letters, was not Stanley but

'Puerto Argentina'. The map stated that the islands were under 'military government', along with South Georgia and the Sandwich Islands. I suppose that meant *Argentinian* military government, because the islands were part of Argentina's most southerly region, the 'National Territory of Tierra del Fuego, Antarctica and the islands of the South Atlantic'.

After we'd checked in, some of the team went to phone home from an international communications office near the hotel (if you phoned from the hotel your bill looked like Argentina's overdraft at the World Bank). On the list of international codes, there was no number for Britain, Great Britain, England or the United Kingdom. It was obviously omitted by official order. It seemed a bit petty, especially when the girls on duty told you without a blink. Ordinary people didn't seem to have a problem dealing with the Brits.

There was something odd about these experiences. Politically nothing was settled. The Argentinians simply knew, as a matter of fact, that the Falklands belonged to them. On a personal level, there was nothing offensive about this claim (nothing all that surprising, either, when you realize how close the islands are). No one throws it in your face, or makes a fuss about it. It makes no difference to the way ordinary Argentinians relate to ordinary English people. But it struck me as a bit odd that we won, they lost, and yet the conditions that led to the war are exactly the same as they always were. If ever another madman were to take over, he could use the same arguments to start the whole thing up all over again . . .

Well, perhaps I had it wrong. I was wrong on practically every other count. The Buenos Aires we saw had little in common with the city I had imagined. The airport was bright, airy, efficient and clean. On the way in from the airport, as open grassy expanses gave way to buildings, there were some areas that were obviously shanty towns, and maybe the outlying suburbs were not up to much. But the road was a newish motorway, and it led straight to the heart of a city that was more like central London or Paris than the poor, blighted, filthy place of my imagination.

A walk around town confirmed my first impressions. The place looked pretty clean, cleaner than London. And the traffic! I was lucky not to be impaled on a bumper. God alive, I thought as I dodged my way over a pedestrian crossing, these Argentinians seem determined to do for me one way or another, if not ten years ago, then now. Mind you, the cars seemed a bit old-fashioned. As far as I could tell, the locally-made ones were mostly Austin Marina bodies with a variety of accessories to give the impression of different makes.

And the shops! There were some places that would make you think you were in Kensington. The buildings are solid, ornate nineteenth-century European style. There's a branch of Harrods, a Cardin, a Gucci, and everything at prices that destroyed any hopes of picking up high-quality stuff cheaply. I thought at least that cheap leather would be easy to come by. This was the land of gauchos and beef. But no; even the leather was much the same price as London, and it was probably the same leather, too.

One thing I was almost right about: the inflation. There *had* been inflation you wouldn't believe – 5,000 per cent. That had meant prices doubling every week. But by some trick, inflation had stopped dead in its tracks a year or so earlier. How had it happened? The people I asked couldn't explain. One man – intelligent, well-travelled, with excellent English – said, 'This is magical realism', and left it at that.

Anyway, no problems. The local currency, the austral, was pegged to the dollar, and everyone was happy to take either dollars or 'australians', as we nicknamed the Argentinian money. The only real difficulty was that the chronic inflation meant that there were 10,000 australians to a dollar. You needed a backpack to carry enough of them to do serious shopping, and a computer brain to remember how many zeros to knock off when working out the exchange.

One thing I will say about Buenos Aires: the women are

gorgeous. They seem to go with the centre of the city – classy, wealthy, sleek, well-dressed. It was impossible to put the world to rights here, at least not when you were spending a happy hour nursing beers at a pavement café. Gary, John and I tried it. I was the soul of discretion, of course, but Gary, in the middle of some anecdote, would break off as if he had just seen a Pucará coming in for the attack. 'Bloody hell,' he would mutter, eyes tracking some vision over my shoulder, 'I could get used to this place.'

One thing I found very odd. On every block there were newspaper kiosks, and almost all of them displayed the most mind-blowing pornographic magazines I have ever seen. It wasn't a question of taking a quick peak behind a curtain – they were right out there for anyone to see. Very odd that such things should exist in a Catholic country, odder still to display them.

This place never seemed to sleep. My room overlooked a main avenue, and the traffic would still be going at three in the morning, horns beeping. Parties would go on till late, and then the shops would open early, with people polishing up the windows and kids hauling crates of Coca-Cola about.

It was hard to realize at first that the atmosphere wasn't always so relaxed. Not so long ago, Argentina had been a police state. Apparently, every Thursday the central square in Buenos Aires was still taken over by the mothers of 'the Disappeared', protesting that even the present government was not doing enough to find relatives spirited away to their deaths over the years of dictatorship, or doing enough to punish those responsible.

Then we heard a story that revealed something of the hidden tensions. A man had been driving along with his ten-year-old son. A policeman stopped him, drew a gun and demanded money. The man refused. The policeman shot him, twice, in front of his son. There were many other witnesses. The next morning the son was on a breakfast TV show that seemed to specialize in gruesome, tear-jerking stories about violent deaths, if possible involving children. It appeared that no one had seen anything after all. No one was prepared to testify against a policeman for fear of what might happen. It was the sort of story, common enough in South America, that made you glad to be living in Britain.

One day, we took a spin round the city in glorious sunshine that threatened to sizzle the skin off the top of my head. The city was a continuous surprise, if only because it was so European. A few huge avenues were named after dates that had something to do with the declaration of Argentinian independence from Spain early last century. One of them has fourteen lanes, which makes it the widest avenue in the world, according to our driver, Oscar. He was full of information – and misinformation. At one point the 9 July Avenue swirls past a huge monolith, a sort of Cleopatra's needle. What was it? 'Oh, that's there so the avenue has something to go round,' Oscar informed us.

We circled a huge park dotted with big trees with exotic blue blossoms – jacaranda trees – and drove past the largest opera house I've ever seen. It takes up a whole block, and seats 3,500 people.

'President Bush was there on his state visit,' said Oscar proudly.

'I didn't know he could sing,' I said.

I was beginning to feel a bit sleepy. There's only so much tourism you can take, especially when it's hot and you've indulged in the local brew the night before. There seemed to be nothing much about the place to show that it was in South America rather than Europe. I was beginning to think fondly of home. Lucy and James. A good English breakfast. Where in Argentina would I find a good sausage or a rasher of bacon?

Then Oscar promised to show off something that would revive my interest – the home of the footballer, Diego Maradona. It turned out to be a massive, modern, angular block of metal, concrete and darkened glass. He lived in *all that*? Well, not exactly. He owned it all, but it was a block of apartments, and he lived in one of them. We didn't call in. It reminded me of what I was missing: a good football match. Now that would be worth staying on for.

At this point, I must have dozed off, because the next I knew we were down by the docks, in a working-class area of old timber and tin shacks, cheerfully painted in greens and reds. One street was obviously set up for tourists, with artists displaying paintings of gymnastic locals performing the tango. A young woman, accompanied by an old man on a guitar, was singing in a wavering voice.

Round the corner was something I really needed: a bar, offering shade and refreshment. It had an odd sign – a cut-throat razor and a pair of scissors. Perhaps it had been a barber's shop once, a sort of Argentinian Sweeney Todd's. It overlooked the dock, which reeked of low-tide mud and was lined with hulks that looked as if they'd been left over from a Second World War movie set. The bar, a simple, two-room place, run by a wiry man with a thin moustache, had walls covered with a strange collection of objects – old 78 records, bits of rigging, and old paper currency promising to pay the bearer huge numbers of noughts.

The owner, Jorge, surprised me by asking me and the lads to write our names on the wall. It seemed an odd request. Had he recognized me from somewhere? For a moment, I was nervous. We were among old enemies, weren't we? And no one was supposed to know I was there. But it was OK. Oscar had let slip that we had fought in the war. Jorge hadn't heard of me, and was delighted we were there precisely because we had fought.

'It was a crazy thing, the war,' he said, as if apologizing for the leaders who had caused such an unnecessary division between friendly peoples. 'I am glad you are here, so we can meet.'

He scrawled on the wall in Spanish: '*Aquí hubieron ex-combatientes Ingleses, amigos nuestros.*' – 'Here were English ex-combatants, friends of ours.'

Gary, John and I set aside our hesitation and signed our names. It was obviously the right thing to do, and was appreciated, because when we came to pay, Jorge wouldn't hear of it. 'It is between friends,' he said.

I sometimes wonder: was that little statement on the wall of a dock-side bar the first public, written sign of reconciliation by ordinary men like us?

We didn't have much time to enjoy Buenos Aires, but there was one evening that proved truly memorable. Well, not memorable in detail, because the details were wiped out in a haze of noise, beer and laughter, but memorable in mood.

We had been filming in a local restaurant, found by Gabriel, a towering, tousle-haired film maker who was helping to organize some of the trickier sequences. The place was filled with wooden tables and beams and dangling plants and nooks and crannies, with a dance-floor to one side.

The filming ended. Drinks arrived. The mood became jovial, not to say a little raucous. Soon, Gary was a little the worse for a few ales, and involved in a deeply earnest discussion with Gabriel. At one point, when Gabriel wrapped a genial arm around his shoulders, he pretended to take offence – 'Now listen. The effing Malvinas are effing British. You effing remember that.' Gabriel responded with a grin and a hug and the gift of a tiny toy guardsman from a collection of toys in a side-cabinet. (Why a restaurant should be selling toys I didn't know.)

Anyway, Gary was mortified. 'What can I do?' he muttered. 'He gave me this – after what I said to him! Got to give him something in return.' Urgent and wild talk about early morning trips to Harrods, and sending for a courier to bring a suitable gift from home – anything. In the end Gary stripped off his T-shirt, and offered it as a gift. Gabriel re-dressed him, and reassured him. All Gabriel wanted was to see us happy. This was thanks enough.

Meanwhile I had got talking to the son of the restaurant owner, who turned out to be a rugby fanatic. Somehow the suggestion arose that I should try to arrange for a team of local teenagers to come down from Wales to play against a similar bunch in Buenos Aires. I was able to take the letter of invitation away with me, and handed it over to the local lads when I got home. This left me with a really good feeling, and strengthened my belief that sport can break down barriers. I just hope it comes off.

On our last evening we were invited to a high-class restaurant, Michelangelo's, which is famous for its tango-dancing cabaret. I knew nothing about the tango, but it was supposed to be worth seeing.

The restaurant was a terrific place, created in the huge brick vaults of what had once been a storage cellar, and then a convent. The vaults had also at some time been used as a torture chamber and a smugglers' den. It was supposed to be haunted. Anyway, it had a great atmosphere.

There are lots of stories about its lurid past, though the pamphlet they give you and the plaques on the walls destroy the mystery of the place. At least, they do if you only read them in the English translation. One story concerns the Ghost of Michelangelo, the spirit of a smuggler who had hidden among the crates, intending to stow away on an outgoing ship. This is his terrifying tale, in the English version:

During the nights, he got on here, or according various, someone one night, intented, using this tunnel to get on board as a stowaway. But being hiden, foll on him many bulks that produced him slowly dead by asphyxial. From there, his spirit goes around permanently in this house. Many nights, he shows his appearance with clear steps, with going up and down the ladders, with permanent mumbles.

After being scared out of my wits by this, you can imagine how reassured I felt to get into the cabaret, a little theatre upstairs that made me think we were in for a strip show. It was like nothing I had ever seen before, live or on film. Accompanied by ageing musicians with mournful expressions, extremely fit men and women performed cowboy dances, doing amazing things with *bolas*, the balls on ropes that gauchos use for tripping up cattle. They swung them in blurs, struck the floor with them, tap-dancing with their high-heeled boots at the same time, in a whirl of limbs and ropes. The star of the evening ended up whirling his balls around so close to his head that he whipped sweat off his brow. This is not a trick I'll be practising in a hurry.

These dances were mixed in with tangos, all in old-fashioned 1930s dress. They always looked discreet at first, but then, when things livened up, the main purpose seemed to be for the boy and girl to entangle limbs and trip each other up. It looked like the mating-dance of two mad octopuses. They wound their legs around each other as if heading for a vicious fall, and then escaped with astonishing speed and flexibility. It was great, but once was enough. I don't think I'll be trying to open a tango bar in Nelson.

Besides, by then my mind wasn't as much on the show as it might have been, because I was distracted by what had happened over the previous three days.

No doubt about it, the purpose of my trip had already been fulfilled, and no number of ball-swinging gauchos or loose-limbed tango dancers would have been able to change my mood.

4

MEETING MY 'TORMENTOR'

17 November 1991

The meeting with the pilot – Carlos Cachon – was to take place in an apartment owned by the parents of one of Malcolm's TV contacts, Claudia – Gabriel's dark-haired and very chic wife. It would be as private, quiet and discreet as was possible, given that we would be meeting in front of cameras.

I was incredibly nervous. I chose some lightweight clothes, because I knew I would be bothered by the heat, then chatted stupidly in the van about anything, just to forget the knot in my stomach. We drove to an area of solid, ornate blocks – one building was an embassy – that wouldn't have been out of place in Kensington. A lift took us up to the apartment. Vanessa, the assistant, rang the doorbell.

The sound of the bell brought a sudden thought: 'Is he *here*?' What if he opened the door? No, that was ridiculous. Besides, I knew that Malcolm would not do that to me. But the thought made me horribly aware of my own nerves. It was not as if I were meeting a monster, or something that would hurt me, but . . .

Yes, it was. That's exactly what it felt like – like being a child in the middle of a nightmare. I knew it wasn't true, I knew it wasn't like that, but the knowledge didn't save me from the feelings.

The door opened. The mood lifted a fraction.

God, what an apartment! Claudia's mother had been born in Russia, and been brought to Argentina as a child after the Revolution. Her family had become rich. They all seemed to be good-looking, widely travelled and multi-lingual. The apartment reflected the life style.

An entrance hall contained an English antique desk covered with two or three dozen silver-framed family photographs. I was led round a corner, past a huge living area. I caught a glimpse of a library, which led into a dining room. An old French tapestry on the wall. Shelves of leather-bound books. Two exotic eastern sculptures of mythical animals. Flowery wallpaper on the ceiling. Great folds of yellow curtain across the windows. Thick, light green carpets, deep chairs. The place seemed to show the finest things that Argentinians could aspire to – rich furnishings, a European heritage, intelligence, education, social standing.

No doubt most Argentinians did not live like this. But it showed how good life could be if the country were properly run. No wonder there was anger at the former leaders for making such a mess of things.

But I wasn't there to admire a rich interior – though I did later – and I was far too nervous to concentrate on it anyway. We went past the living area, on along the white-painted corridor, round a corner – this place was a maze – and into a smaller room, a study overlooking a private garden. There, the film crew was all set up, lights and cameras ready. Outside the picture window was a balcony enclosed in wire, either to keep children in or thieves out, perhaps both. A solid leather sofa, with bookshelves on either side. An *Encyclopædia Britannica*, and rows of *National Geographic*s.

I sat down, and took a sip of mineral water, wondering what on earth was going to happen next. Brian, the cameraman, did some shots of me sitting down. I stood up, paced around, drank some more water. Of course, the whole thing had been carefully planned. The pilot had been collected, and was waiting nearby until I was in position, and the cameras were rolling.

You might think it was an artificial setting for such an emotional meeting. True, there have been many times I have felt as if I was being pinned down and examined by scientists. But not at that moment. I was so wound up I couldn't think of anything except the immediate future, and that was blank. I was frightened of how I might react if the pilot turned out to be a cold fish, with no emotion in his eyes and no soul. I wondered if I were about to make an idiot of myself, even disgrace myself by doing something stupid. If he were to try to make everything all right with some glib remark, I knew I wouldn't be able to restrain myself. I'd walk out, ruin the film, ruin my friendship with Malcolm, destroy my chances of coming to terms with the past, take back home the burden I had brought . . .

The crew made cheery remarks, and I tried to pretend I was being the true professional. But I wasn't. My mouth was dry. I could have done with a beer – anything – to relax me. It reminded me of being a kid, waiting to see the headmaster, knowing something was going to happen, probably going to get the cane, but not sure what for.

And then, there was the assistant producer and interpreter, Benetta, showing in my 'tormentor'. But he didn't look like a tormentor. He didn't look much like a pilot, not at all like a man with the power to kill forty-seven men and injure ninety-seven others. He was shorter than me, athletic-looking, but very much lighter build than me, with brown puppy-dog eyes and a moustache. I thought: I could crush this little guy.

He looked at me, and I could see the shock. He sort of held back, just for an instant. I thought at the time it was the shock of seeing what he had done to me.

I felt a sudden rush of anger. It was as if the sight of him suddenly opened the doors to past experience. Not that the memories themselves came pouring through – there was too much else going on for that. But it was as if I knew they were there, and this man was the key to them, and the pain. This was the man who had caused the flash that singed off my eyelids, the fire that scorched my skin and burned away my hands, the man who had done as much, and worse, to my mates, who had changed my life and ruined scores of others. I didn't want to remember – I had come here to put the memories behind me, once and for all – but here he was, the man who had recreated my life, threatening me with the past I had come here to forget, expecting me to treat him like some kind of a friend. There was a part of me – Simon Weston, the twenty-year-old Welsh Guard squaddie – that wanted to hate him, needed to hate him. I saw how small he was, how insignificant; I saw how easily I could smash in his face.

He came forward with his hand out, eager for the meeting.

Carlos was the son of a rep. who sold the products of a factory in the south, in Mar del Plata. They weren't a rich family, but Carlos was bright enough to consider becoming a doctor. When he was sixteen, and about to start the long business of medical training, one of his friends decided to try for the Air Force. Carlos went along to keep him company, just for fun, not with any idea of committing himself to a new career.

Not long afterwards, a letter arrived informing him that he had passed the Air Force tests. Ironically, his friend had failed. On impulse, Carlos gave up his plans for a medical career, and accepted the offer. He qualified as a pilot in the early 1970s, when he was approaching thirty.

By then his life had taken another turn. On his seventeenth birthday, just after he started his Air Force training, he was invited to a party where he met a petite, dark-eyed fourteen-year-old. Her name was Graciela. The next morning, he was feeling so groggy from too many vodka-and-Cokes that he could remember nothing much except her name and the fact that she was extremely pretty. That was enough. He tracked her down through a mutual friend, and began to date her. They were married six years later. So they almost grew up together. Or rather, as Graciela put it, 'we stopped growing together'.

When the war broke out, Graciela and their two young children, a boy aged five and a girl aged three, were living in a military apartment in San Luis province, in central Argentina, while Carlos, now a first lieutenant, was in Río Gallegos in the south, the closest Air Force base to the Falklands, 350 miles due east.

It was a tense time. Carlos would give Graciela a daily phone call to tell her he was all right, but he could not divulge any details. They were just brief calls – 'I'm all right. How are you?' – 'We're fine' – nothing but simple reassurances. Until the call arrived, though, she had no idea if he had come through that day unscathed.

Once, before the time of the daily call, Graciela was returning from a shopping trip when she saw the local priest stop outside her apartment block. The block contained four flats, two up and two down. She and the children lived upstairs, to the left. She guessed what the visit meant: one of the four men whose families lived there had been killed. Her heart in her mouth, she watched him. He started to climb the stairs. For a terrible moment she thought he had come for her. Then she saw him turn right, not left . . . She was seized by a wave of relief that she had been spared, and horror that her friend's husband was dead.

Carlos had flown two missions before the day of the raid on the *Sir Galahad*. His 5th Hunter Group – initially twelve Skyhawk A4Bs – flew over 100 sorties during the war, sinking three ships and damaging six others. It was dangerous and demanding business. In all, ten Skyhawks were shot down and nine of the group's pilots killed. They had to come in so low and so fast that there was always a risk of doubt about identification. On 1 May 1982, when the British forces were expected any day, Carlos had bombed one of his own ships, the cargo vessel *Formosa*. Luckily, the bomb didn't explode – 'Intelligent bomb!' he commented with a wry smile when he told the story later. (Frequently bombs failed to explode, because the planes dropped them when so close to their targets that they didn't have time to prime themselves. If it hadn't been for this, we would have lost many more ships.) On another occasion, he was about to bomb a British ship when he saw that it was the hospital ship *Uganda*, and pulled away just in time.

On the day of the *Sir Galahad* bombing – 8 June – there were eight Skyhawks in his flight. It was chilly, with scattered clouds and showers. The planes were each laden with three 250kg bombs – not a full load, but they needed extra fuel for the trip. During the forty-minute flight out to the islands, they would refuel over the ocean, at about the half-way point. Three of the planes had problems refuelling, and had to turn back. They included the flight leader. The task of leading the squadron now fell to Carlos, flying only his third war mission. He heard the order come over his headphones – 'You're in command! Take them to glory!' – and felt a thrill of fear. Later he was to find this reassuring. 'No one who is normal would be unafraid. Now at least I know I'm normal!'

The mission was clear enough: he was to attack ships lying in Port Fitzroy, one of the two parallel inlets to the south of Stanley. He came in fast from the south-west, flying low, to avoid the British radar. The height, the speed and a succession of localized but violent rainstorms wiped out all fear and kept him at a peak of concentration. He spotted Port Fitzroy, zoomed over the inlet from the west, and . . .

No ships! He had been wrongly briefed. Banking hard over the sea, he headed south, and was already on his way home in his mind, when: 'There they are!' came a voice over his headphones, referring to two grey shapes, *Sir Tristram* and *Sir Galahad*, lying to the west, in Port Pleasant. He banked again, lined up on the *Sir Galahad*, dropped down to within a few feet of the surface, and came at us.

At that moment, I had just been asked to get a cup of tea by Corporal Pemberton. 'Ah, come on, Pem, ask someone else will you?' I said. If only I'd done as I was told. That's what you get for disobeying orders. It was then that I started jogging back along the deck to slap Yorkie awake, and heard warnings being shouted.

After a few seconds over open water, Carlos released all three bombs. By the time one of them struck, engulfing me and a hundred others in flames, he was pulling up over the ship, and aiming for home. He had no idea if the bombs had actually exploded – he couldn't look behind him to check – but he was certain, absolutely certain, he had hit his target. There was no way he could have missed. He felt a surge of exhilaration. He had achieved what he had been training for, and as he said, 'In war that's all that matters.'

Radio silence on the flight back meant he had no idea if he had been successful or not until he landed. Then one of the others who had been behind him congratulated him: '*¡Bueno impacto!*' There was no rejoicing. His commander, who had known him for ten years, merely said: 'I would have expected nothing less from you.'

The exhilaration did not last. The war was over a week later, and he had to come to terms with defeat, the death of friends and political upheaval.

And there was more. He knew his bombs had wrought terrible damage, and it bothered him. A week after his return he began to get cramps in his back, and he would wake in the early hours in pain. The pain shifted to his mind. He felt an emptiness that could only be filled by knowledge of the effects of his action.

Only years later did he begin to find what he was looking for. He saw a photograph of the *Sir Galahad* in flames, and was horrified. But he never knew how many people had been killed or injured. For years he had wanted to meet someone from the other side, if possible someone from the *Sir Galahad*, to express his sympathy, make a human contact, find the human face behind the smoke and flames. Much later, he even saw a picture of me, though he had no reason to remember my name. This strengthened both his feeling of horror and his need to make contact, to be able to speak to a British person and explain that he had not acted out of anger or bitterness, that there had not been anything personal in his action.

So when Malcolm approached him, it was like an answer to a prayer, or, in his words, 'It was like touching heaven with my hands.' He had left the Air Force years earlier to earn a better living as a salesman, working as an agent for a manufacturer of packaging and boxes. He and his family had returned to an apartment in Mar del Plata, where his parents came from. Malcolm not only convinced him that the film was going to tell a little of the truth about the war – something that had been avoided in Argentina – but he also offered the chance of finding some kind of release, a minor version of the kind of release I was seeking.

So when he came in and looked at me, the shock I saw in him was not the shock of revulsion at seeing a burned face, but the shock of recognition. There was a human face behind the flames he had caused, and he had already seen it.

His hesitation when he saw me lasted only a second. Then he held out his hand.

The rage that was building up in me was only part of what I felt, though it took a long time for me to begin to understand my own confused and compressed feelings.

Those were not the eyes of a killer. There was a warmth in them, a sadness, a sincerity, and a trust that I would not have betrayed even if we had been alone. Although one part of me felt the surge of anger, instantly other parts of me rushed to control it. I don't think any flicker of what I was feeling showed in my expression or actions.

I took his hand. 'Hello,' I said.

'Hello. How are you?' he replied, in English. 'Nice to see you.'

The contact brought a sense of relief. The same hand that had released the bomb into the side of the *Galahad* was in mine; yet this man I called my tormentor, as if he was some sort of sadistic giant, had a gentleness about him. He felt the clawed fingers and the lump in the middle of my palm, but there was no look of surprise or shock on his face.

I let go his hand.

The rage was still there. But I would never have forgiven myself if I had given in to it, because I knew how wrong it would have been. It was OK to feel the anger; but it was good – very good – to know that I was in control. Simon Weston, the twenty-year-old squaddie, was long gone. I was a thirty-year-old husband and father, with ten years of change and experience behind me, and whatever I had become, it was not all bad, and the man sitting down beside me was part of that change.

It was Carlos who spoke first. He had something to say, and he wanted to say it in English. He looked at me, 'I'm sorry . . .'

'Don't be sorry,' I said quickly. I was afraid he was about to apologize for his actions. No apology was necessary – or possible. If he tried to, I was afraid my anger would explode after all.

' . . . for you and your family,' he went on.

At once, tension ebbed. That was not an apology, but an expression of sympathy.

'Well, maybe so, but you didn't do it on purpose,' I told him. 'You didn't do it deliberately, to me personally.'

He stared at me. I had reached the limit of his English.

'*Yo entiendo* . . . I understand English . . . more or less . . .' he hesitated, and Benetta began to interpret.

This released Carlos to give a little formal speech of welcome, and then, without thinking, I began to speak. I had no plan of what I was going to say, only a general idea that I wanted to ask a couple of specific questions about the raid. As it turned out, I didn't get around to these for a while. I told him I hadn't come here to shock him or give him a hard time, that all I wanted was to put to bed some ghosts inside me, that this was probably the only way I could complete my grieving. I hoped he understood.

He didn't, and it was too long a speech to come across well in translation. Neither of us was used to talking through an interpreter. We never learned to slow down, or to talk in small speeches. Poor Benetta was fighting to hold an avalanche of words in her head. The messages Carlos and I were trying to send each other were in constant danger of being lost.

No, Carlos wasn't shocked. He was pleased. He said he'd wanted for years to meet someone who'd had a far harder time than he had. He said the war was an accident for him as well as for me, and that this was an opportunity to erase scars and grief.

Good sentiments. I warmed towards him. I could feel the resentments of the last ten years beginning to slip away. He was just an ordinary bloke, after all. There was no anger left now, only a desire to make him understand why I had wanted this meeting, why I had wanted to make contact, person to person.

'This is a time when men who fought can say "Ten years is enough." We shouldn't be allowing politicians or politics to stop us from being human beings. We have to say, "It's over." It's over. I don't blame you for what happened, although you led the attack. I don't blame you for that, as I know that in war nothing is personal. It can't be.'

With hardly a pause, I plunged on, expressing sympathy for him as a friend of grieving families, and for the families themselves, and saying I hoped the documentary would contribute to better understanding between us all.

It was too much. My words were getting through, but I could see that my feelings were being lost in translation.

Still, he responded. His heart was in the right place. He said, yes, it was true, he'd been on a job, and had been well prepared for it, 'but it is now our responsibility to regain some human value from it all, and neutralize the consequences of what had happened.' That's why this was an important moment; we could work together for reconciliation.

I wasn't so sure about this. I was there for my own reasons. I didn't want to get into things like reconciliation between nations.

'I think it's a responsibility of ordinary people,' he went on, 'to help our diplomats to break down the barriers that lead to war . . .'

Perhaps so, but I would feel easier if we could talk about more down-to-earth matters. Besides, it was the end of a reel. There was a brief break. Carlos chatted in Spanish to Benetta, and seemed to gain in confidence. Then I brought the conversation back to us. Had it been hard for him to come here?

No, no, no. For many years he had wanted to meet someone he'd fought against. A dream had been realized.

In turn, he asked me how my life had been since the accident. A considerate man was Carlos, but where could I begin? Best not try. Best stick to the present.

'Bloody hard!' I said with feeling. 'But I don't think it could have been harder than coming to meet you today. Not so much for me, but because I know that the families and the loved ones of my friends and my comrades who were injured will see this. I just hope they will be able to take away from this film a feeling of tolerance.'

I don't know where the idea of 'tolerance' came from, but it suddenly seemed a key to a lot of things. I wanted many people to show tolerance: me in my response to Carlos, the families at home in their response to both of us, the British and Argentinian governments in response to each other.

On I went: there was no blame on either side . . . We, too, were only servicemen doing our jobs . . . Nothing I could say would take away his grief . . . This was doing a lot to relieve my own personal anguish . . . I didn't know where I was going with all this, and I couldn't even remember having said it afterwards, but, at last, in my own way, I was getting to the core of it.

I said I hoped the film and the book would allow people to see Carlos as a person, as I was doing right then. 'One of the things I wanted to do,' I went on, 'was to look at you and see if you had life in your eyes, because, believe me, in the last ten years, I've wondered – I've really wondered. And there *is* life in your eyes, and you're *not* the spectre that's been haunting me.'

Benetta was going crazy trying to make notes and keep up with me, and she did brilliantly. She spoke for as long as I had done, and when I heard the word *fantasma* – spectre, ghost – I knew she had captured what I wanted to say.

I don't know if Carlos had really understood. He was talking about the Argentinians believing the war to be rooted in a just cause, and remembering the heroes of the war, and the need to get beyond that, to the human, and the personal . . .

Perhaps my attention was beginning to wander, or perhaps I was beginning to get a little impatient, for I suddenly switched to a technical point. 'How did the intelligence people know that my ship was where it was?'

He didn't know. He had just been told the ships were there. But it led, he continued, to a 'difficult, sad moment'.

The understatement of the decade! 'Carnage,' I told him. 'As bad as it could ever get for any human beings.' But I didn't want to dwell on the horrors. He could see well enough what it had been like from my face.

Had been like – that was the point. Past tense. If we were to put the war aside, there had to be some give and take, a little humour. I told him that he and his men had been good pilots – even the British pilots had complimented them. 'You could do your job well. I wish you hadn't been able to map-read so well!'

A laugh, then back to another specific question: had all his men got back safely? Yes, they had, though the next mission – arriving at the Falklands when we were ready for them – had lost all of its eight Skyhawks. (In all, the Argentinians had lost seventy-five planes.)

I sympathized with him. He had lost friends, as I had. We were both losers. 'Although Britain was seen to win the conflict, nobody won,' I said. 'We have the victors and the vanquished, but there's nothing victorious in what happened – just a great deal of sadness.' The best the Falklands War could achieve was to force negotiations – a hollow conclusion, when negotiations would have been better from the start. 'If more people were willing to face up to their fears, the way we are meeting today, perhaps none of it would have been necessary, and you would still have your friends and I would still have mine.'

War was a terrible thing, I continued. We both knew that. Would Carlos let his kids join the armed forces?

Yes. Carlos would be happy if his son were to choose the forces as a career, happy whatever choice he makes, as long as it is done with honour. This was the only way to act, in whatever circumstances.

Honour seemed to be super-important to him. At the time, as a pilot, he had had no choice. Honour lay in doing what he had done. Now, though, it was possible to find honour in a different type of action, by influencing politicians to talk to each other. 'I believe in my soul that those islands belong to Argentina, and perhaps you feel equally strongly that they are British, but that need not enter into the relationship between us.'

We were getting into a difficult area, because he was forgetting a point I felt strongly about. In fact, it was the core of the whole dispute, as far as I was concerned, and it inspired me to make the longest speech of the afternoon. I suppose I felt there were some principles at stake on my side as well.

The question had to come down to a choice by the people who lived there. He would surely understand that. 'You're re-experiencing democracy and freedom, which is wonderful ... In Buenos Aires, you can see people with a great deal of freedom and a great deal of happiness, and I don't think anybody had a right to take that away. If any one person were to take the rights of the other away, I think that would be wrong. Ultimately, that's what I believe I was there for – to protect the freedoms, the democracy of those people who live there.'

As I often do when I'm trying to make a strongly-held point, I began to repeat myself: 'I believed that it was right then, and I still believe it was right to react in the way that we did, and I still believe that the solution that we ended up with was the only right one, because *nobody* has the right to take anything by force.'

Then suddenly I saw another dimension to the question of ownership. How could a country 'own' land that was not its own? I started to become philosophical: 'Ultimately none of us owns anything,' I continued, 'because we come into this world with nothing, and we go out of it with nothing, so we've owned nothing, we've just enjoyed it for the time we were here.'

I paused. I wouldn't get anywhere with this. Back to practical-ities. 'I honestly believe that if we're ever to resolve the differences over the Falklands, we have to get the people who so-called matter – the politicians – round a table.' That at least we could agree on. 'But ultimately the decision on who has sovereignty has to come down to the people who live there, and call the place their home. That's the way I feel about it, and those are the reasons I was there.'

Probably I should have stopped there, but other thoughts came to me, in a steady stream. Argentina claims we stole the islands in the first place, but that means we're going back a couple of centuries, and what happened then can hardly have any bearing ... At this point, luckily, the film ran out, and I sat back, exhausted, uncomfortably warm with the lights and the concentration, and let Benetta do her best.

I hope she spared him. I doubt if we would ever have agreed on the question of sovereignty. Each of us claimed to be for 'democracy', just as everybody believes he or she is on the side of good or has a sense of humour, but we still wouldn't have agreed. I believed in the rights of the Falklanders. He would have said that as the land was Argentinian, it was the people of Argentina who should decide. Deadlock. It was best to avoid it. Arguing would solve nothing, and no one would care anyway.

But at least we were on firm ground about the futility of war and the need for contacts. When we started up again, we were on to easier, more personal topics – kids, and the importance of sport. 'I just hope that if our sons ever meet,' I said, 'it will be on a field of sport and not of combat, and that they can enjoy a beer, a *cerveza*, after the game. And it won't matter who wins or loses on that day.'

I was beginning to feel we had gone as far as we could, and found myself working up to a finale, speaking about my hopes that such pain should never be experienced again, and the role of our kids in making sure that it wouldn't be, and not wishing Carlos any evil, and hoping there would be a decent political solution that everyone could be pleased with, including the Falklanders.

The heat was beginning to build up more under the lights, and I was looking forward to a drink. There was only one more thing to be said. 'I certainly won't forget this moment. It's done a lot for me – *what* I don't know, but it's done something already . . . I hope that you enjoy the rest of your life, because I think that after this meeting, I certainly will, and I wish you all the best. Take care.'

There. That was it. I shook his hand again, and waited impatiently for Benetta to finish interpreting. But Carlos wasn't ready to stop yet. Perhaps touching my hand again sparked a new thought. '¡*Mira, Simon!*' – 'Look, Simon!' – he said. It was the first time he'd used my name. He did so, I think, because he suddenly needed to acknowledge my injuries directly. 'Look, Simon . . . You may have discovered over the last few years that there are in your body things more important than your hands. Your mind, your heart, your eyes, which are expressive, your mouth which can express feelings – those things are all more important than your hands. I think it's a disability you have already overcome.'

Nice thought. Now it really was time to end, and I said so with a glance at Malcolm.

No. Carlos had started again, expressing the hope that this would not be our last meeting. I played this suggestion a little cool. It was a long way to come, so it was really in the lap of the gods.

'That's about it,' I said again. 'I can't say any more.'

Carlos, too, relaxed. He mentioned football, and rugby. He said he played rugby – full back. I'd been a prop forward, and pointed out my greatest qualification – 'No neck!' We agreed it would be a good thing if more conflicts could be settled by sport.

'Perhaps in a thousand years we'll evolve to that point,' he said with a laugh, but the laughter was becoming a little forced on both sides.

'All right. That's it.' I looked at Malcolm: why the hell was he still filming?

'*Bien*. Let's go.' Carlos knew it was over, too. We both stood up awkwardly.

'Yeah, I think so.' And then to Malcolm again: 'I think you've seen the end. Are you satisfied?'

'It's your meeting,' he said, from beside the camera.

I was at a bit of a loss. The camera was still running, and the heat of the lights was killing me. 'What are we doing now? Have you got some coffee lined up or something?'

'Whatever you want to do.'

'Let's have a cup of coffee because I'm parched.'

'He was trying to give you an invitation earlier,' Malcolm said.

'An invitation to what?'

'To meet.'

I was confused. I knew that there was a plan for the other lads to meet up with their opposite numbers, and that perhaps I was expected to be part of that. But I wasn't too clear about what exactly would happen, or what my role might be. There simply hadn't been time to think about it.

Just then the idea of an invitation didn't register because there was a brief flurry of words in Spanish and English, and before I knew it the suggestion was made that Carlos should introduce his wife. I didn't know she was there until that moment.

At this I could feel a part of me – the old, unreconstructed Simon Weston – really backing off. I wasn't there for social reasons. I really didn't have all that much interest in meeting Carlos's wife. I had got what I wanted from the meeting. Not that it was a big deal. I certainly wasn't going to be anything but polite.

Then I realized: the camera was still running. At this point I began to feel the whole thing was getting out of hand. Meeting Carlos's wife had nothing to do with the relationship between me and Carlos. It was tacky. More than that, it might actually detract from the meeting in some way. 'Do we need to film this?' I asked.

Malcolm nodded.

'Why?'

'It's what's happening.'

'I know it's what's happening, but *why*? I don't mind meeting his wife, but . . .' I saw Malcolm's face. He was going to go on filming, no matter what, unless I threw a tantrum. I had seen enough to know that. And, damn his eyes, I respected him enough and trusted him enough to respect my wishes, even then, to let him do it. And he knew it.

Purely not to offend Carlos, I gave in: 'Oh, yeah, go on – go fetch her.' Carlos vanished, and Malcolm took the opportunity to probe me about the meeting. Well, I felt good about the meeting, and said so. But was I relieved? How could I answer that truthfully?

I didn't have to. Carlos was ushering in Graciela. I had to admit it, she was a real charmer – petite, even smaller than Carlos, with coal-dark eyes and short, straight hair. '*Es Simon*,' Carlos said.

I shook her hand.

'*Simon*,' she said. '*¿Qué tal?*'

We started a stilted conversation, the three of us, with Benetta's help. For the first time Carlos asked about my private life. 'Your wife,' he asked in English, 'in London?'

I explained that she was in Liverpool right then, with my little boy's grandmother, but that we lived in Wales.

Carlos asked their names. I told him. He told me how long he and Graciela had been married. We all agreed that time marches on, and that this was all very nice etc., but what we really needed was a beer or three, because it really was *very* hot in there.

And still the camera ran.

Then I found myself chatting about the politics of the Falklands again, which was not something I had ever wanted to get into, so I brought the conversation back to the two of us – Carlos and me – and the frustration of not being able to be more relaxed together. 'It's language, that's all that separates us now.'

Graciela nodded. 'We have to promise that for the next time we'll have to learn to communicate.'

'If you come to my house,' Carlos added, 'and you're not speaking Spanish, I won't give you anything to eat!'

I laughed. 'Nothing to eat! Oh, boy! That's a major problem!'

Then Carlos surprised me by offering me a little Argentinian

Air Force calendar marking the tenth anniversary of the war. It contained twelve pictures honouring, not to say glorifying, the role of the Air Force. He leafed through it for me: a Pucará blowing up a helicopter at Goose Green, a Mirage engaging Sea Harriers, Skyhawks attacking the *Coventry*, and – for September – a view of Carlos in his Skyhawk blowing up the *Sir Galahad*.

'That's us. The *Galahad*,' I said. 'Thank you.' I doubt if I kept the irony out of my voice. It was a very strange present. I mean, if you had almost killed someone by mistake, would you give him a picture of the deed? It was so strange that I forgot about it instantly. Call it an emotional defence mechanism; call it instant forgiveness, because I'm sure he meant no offence. He happily handed out the same calendars to everyone, with obvious pleasure. Anyway, I somehow managed to lose mine very soon afterwards.

Now it really was over. We all wanted something to eat and drink, and there was nothing else to say. It had all happened in slow motion, like a dream, when all the time my feelings had been tripping over themselves to get out. There were things I still needed to say on camera, so while the other two moved away, down the corridor, I stayed on and spoke about my feelings – my initial anger, and then my immense relief at having met Carlos – to Malcolm, and to the camera.

But there were other hurdles yet, before I could relax into the sense of relief.

For one thing, as we were talking afterwards in the gorgeous sitting-room, Graciela and Carlos actually invited me to stay in their apartment in Mar del Plata. I was well out of that. My emotions were so overburdened I could hardly take anything more. Certainly the idea of *staying* with them was too much.

Luckily, it was not up to me. Our schedule was just too tight, and I was able to refuse graciously.

Then, when the time came to say goodbye, Carlos took

me completely by surprise. He wrapped his arms round my shoulders and hugged me. God, that gave me real problems. I'm not a hugging sort of person, and I don't know people who make a habit of hugging. Hugging women is one thing, but hugging men? Well, it's not me, or part of my culture.

On top of this, all my old worries about meeting Carlos came rushing up inside me. I had already shaken hands with the man who had killed my friends, and I was as certain as I could be that their families would not thank me for it. I had spent two hours talking to him, face to face, man to man, without expressing the grief and anger the families must feel. They wouldn't thank me for this either. But at least they – or some of them – might understand my reasons for wanting the meeting. What I was sure that they would find impossible to accept was any sign that I could instantly forgive and forget. That's what the hug signified for me. It was not something I could do.

Yet, on another level, I liked him. The warmth, the sincerity, the depth of sadness, the shared experiences as husband and father, the shared experience of being caught up in the vast machinery of warfare – all this had drawn us together as human beings.

So, rather than reject him, I allowed him to hug me, and found myself responding – clumsily, without any depth of feeling, but still responding. It was either this, or push him away, and after what we'd been through that would have been wrong as well. I thought: thank God it's not on film.

There was a lot to work through. For me, that takes time. I'm not good at putting feelings into words instantly. But one thing was certain: once I was out of the apartment, back in the hotel, having a beer with the lads, I felt as if a huge weight had been lifted from me.

I was thankful that the strain of the meeting was over, of course, but it was more than that. It felt like the strangest thing, as if I were flying, as if I had been suddenly reprieved from a life sentence, as if suddenly someone had given me the most wonderful present.

I made a start at getting to grips with all this immediately after the meeting with Carlos, when I was talking to Malcolm. I talked of my initial desire to find something to hate in Carlos, my discovery of his professionalism and his humanity, the strangeness of discovering that the man who had caused so much damage to me should have a wife and family, the extraordinary difference I felt between 'before' and 'after', between 'then' and 'now'.

A chapter of my life was now finished. I had changed – I could feel it already. I was pleased with the realization that I had controlled my anger. I felt a new tolerance growing in me, especially towards Carlos. I could see that what he had done was a limited part of his life. There was so much more to him than being a fighter pilot who had bombed a ship ten years earlier. I had seen my tormentor, and I was free of him.

'I hope they'll understand,' I said to Malcolm, and to the camera, speaking to the public and the people back home whose reactions I feared. 'It's not about politics, it's not about money, it's not about being unfaithful to the families, or to the memories of my friends and colleagues who died. It's about me, Simon Weston, the man, the person, the human being who is dealing with his own problems his own way, because he had an opportunity to do these things. I hope people will be more tolerant with me than perhaps I have been with myself for the last ten years.'

Yes, I could afford to be kinder to myself, and to others, from now on. No need any more to force myself to carry the burden of the past. Never again need I fear facing anybody. I said it was as if I had been holding myself to ransom for years, 'not ever meeting the person who held your body in torment'.

Then, as I thought back over the day, it struck me what an odd image this was. It confused Carlos with me. Should I believe what I almost said: that I, not Carlos, was the tormentor I had been longing to escape? I seemed to have come all this way to find Carlos, and succeeded in finding not just him but a new self as well.

Whatever it was that had been oppressing me, I was free of it, and I felt great. Now I wanted to get away from Argentina, on to the Falklands to meet whatever awaited me there, and then hurry home.

5

THE RANCH

19–20 November 1991

Two days later, there was to be a different kind of meeting – a group meeting between English and Argentinian veterans. It was to take place at a country estate belonging to Gabriel, our fixer. Carlos would be there, along with Gary and John's opposite numbers, one of whom had fought on Tumbledown, the other on Wireless Ridge.

Admittedly it would extend the range and significance of the film, but I really didn't want anything to do with it. If I had felt good the previous night, it was nothing to how I felt the following morning. I felt so good I found it hard to believe, and harder still to put into words. There was something magical about the feeling, something mysterious. I simply knew that my release from the past was almost complete, and there was nothing in the future that I couldn't handle – good or bad.

This was the feeling I wanted to be left with. I didn't want to be bothered with anything else, and certainly not the business of once again being at the centre of attention. I knew that's what would happen, not just because I look different, but because it would look good on film.

There was another reason for me not to be part of the meeting.

Gary and John had begun to share their pasts with me. They had had much more experience of war than me, and I enjoyed hearing what they had seen and done. So it seemed only fair that they get as much out of all this as possible. When they met their opposite numbers, the mood would be totally different from the meeting between Carlos and me. No one in that group would have the emotional burdens I had – and Carlos had. They would be discussing their military experiences. That was how it should be. It would spoil it all for them if I were to come barging in. I had made my decision. 'I'll be fine wandering round in town,' I told Malcolm. He was not happy, because he had some idea of the sequence of shots he wanted, and it included me.

No way. What had I got to gain from meeting Carlos again? I had achieved the peace I had come to find. I didn't want to risk undoing the good work of Sunday. Carlos held no further interest for me. It was as simple as that.

Malcolm knew me better than to try to make me change my mind, but he asked me if I would go along in the car, just so that we could be filmed arriving as a group. After that, if I didn't want to be included, that was up to me. Fair enough. I couldn't see the point of it, but I owed him all the help I could give, as long as it didn't undermine my own peace of mind. Besides, when I thought about it, I didn't mind going along for the ride. This would be my first – and perhaps only – trip outside Buenos Aires.

Still feeling a little wary, but nevertheless determined to stick to my decision, I joined the others for the trip into the countryside.

It gave me a glimpse of a world very different from the sophisticated centre of the capital, of something rather more in line with my preconceived ideas about Argentina. Old colonial houses and modern blocks gave way to shanties, the motorway gave way to an ordinary road, populated by noisy, ramshackle trucks, cheerful bulbous-nosed buses and old jalopies. The countryside was green and lush, but no one seemed to care for it much. The cars, the roads, the houses in the few villages we went through – everything had a rough, unfinished look about it. It wasn't surprising, really, when you considered the huge size of the country in relation to the size of its population – ten times the size of Britain and only half the number of people. I hadn't realized how big it was. The distance we travelled that day hardly showed up on my map.

About thirty miles into the country, we pulled in past a line of dusty houses. There was a line of cars with plastic bottles on their roofs – our driver said this meant that the cars were for sale. Down a side road, where grimy children seemed to be playing near an open sewer, I caught a glimpse through the doorway of a tin shack. Two women were sitting silently looking at a child on a table in front of them. I don't know what they were doing, but the scene – the filthy children, the sewer, the tin shack, the little silent group – was a picture of abject poverty. Opposite was a railway with a fine old engine that looked as if it was a survivor from the 1930s.

Lunch-time. Led by our assistant, Vanessa, we trooped into the weirdest restaurant I'd ever seen. It was like stepping into a shadowy old junk shop. The high walls were covered with a wild collection of objects: the heads of an ostrich, an ant-eater and a boar, snake-skins, old telephones, a radio set, a telescope, whips, a model ship with a dragon's mouth, old rifles, and ancient advertisements for stage shows; there was even a stuffed frog holding a little guitar. From the roof swung a chandelier made of a wagon wheel, with ostrich-eggs dangling from it.

Vanessa thought it was fascinating, but I looked around at the dusty objects, and the dusty bar and tables, and thought: if I want to eat in a pigpen, I'd rather find one for myself. I began to wonder if I was going to survive . . .

. . . especially when we were given the opportunity to try the local delicacy. A plate appeared, piled high with little bits of grilled meat. Now, I've done a bit of travelling and I know that sometimes you are offered things that should never be eaten. I know for instance that it's more than your life is worth to eat mutton-bird in New Zealand, although the Maoris consider it a great delicacy. I had a feeling this was another of those occasions.

Yes: those tasty-looking little morsels were the saliva glands of cows. Thanks, but no thanks. I had the queasy feeling that one bite of saliva gland, and I'd be up on the wall along with the armadillos and the snake-skins. I'm sure I was right, too. The following day a lot of our group went down with severe cases of Galtieri's revenge. It was entirely their own fault. They should never have eaten bits of a cow that were never intended to be eaten. Luckily, the restaurant did a very tasty steak and chips, and the local ale wasn't at all bad.

We carried on into wilder regions, turning off the main road into an unpaved side road. We rattled along, sending a cloud of dust up over scrubby pastures. We passed the rusty wrecks of several cars; they looked as if they had broken down, and had simply never been collected for repair. A swampy area had been used as a rubbish-tip. There was a scummy pool of water in the middle, in which three grimy-looking kids were fishing. I wondered why such an empty area had to be so messy.

Off up another side road – this whole farming area seemed to be divided by a grid of dirt roads – and then into the entrance of a dirt driveway, at the end of which stood two houses surrounded by trees. Several cars and vans were parked in the driveway. I spotted the film crew, ready for us, and beyond, across a lawn and in the shade under more trees, tables and chairs. A crowd of people waited, among them the Argentinian ex-soldiers whom Gary and John were to meet – and, I supposed, Carlos.

Well, I didn't want to know. I had made my decision, and I was going to stick to it. The cameras turned towards us; Gary and John got out. I stayed in the van, and relaxed, without even watching as they strolled over to the meeting.

I was on my own, and all attention was somewhere else – it was great. My mind drifted over the meeting with Carlos and how I felt about it. I could see the two houses through the trees, one belonging to the owner of the farm, the other where the farm hands lived. Nearby was a barn and the wreck of an old tractor. It was very peaceful beneath those trees. They were very tall and were covered with a loose sort of bark that was peeling away from the trunks. I wondered vaguely if the locals had some use for the bark. Silence, except for the buzz of a fly in the midday heat.

I sank into myself. The pressures I had felt from Malcolm and my resentment at being here vanished. I felt again, even more strongly, the extraordinary feeling of release from tension. It wasn't a question of forgiving Carlos for what had happened, because there was nothing to forgive. I had been right: he had only been doing his job, and any professional – me included – would have done the same in those circumstances. Nothing to blame him for, nothing to forgive.

I could see that he was a good man – a man whom I couldn't possibly hate, a man whom I couldn't help liking. No, 'liking' was the wrong word – I couldn't bring myself to say I liked someone who had done what he had done. Besides, liking can only come from really getting to know someone, and Carlos and I had only exchanged a few stilted speeches through Benetta.

Still, I had achieved what I had come for. I had at last seen through impersonal horror, and found a human being. All sadness, worry and guilt had fallen from me.

A strange image came to my mind, something I had heard about and never understood, something to do with Zen Buddhism: the sound of one hand clapping. It hadn't made sense before, and it didn't make sense then, certainly not to someone who's idea of perfection was a perfect pass or a perfect goal, but there was something about the image that fitted my mood.

Afterwards, when I got home, I discovered that the image did after all make a strange sort of sense. Apparently one way to pose the problem is like this: what is the proper response when asked 'What is the sound of one hand clapping?' The proper response is to extend your hand in friendship. That was what Carlos and I had done. Perhaps only a Zen master could describe the feeling of release that we experienced.

I felt everything had been changed. The past was slipping away, and I could look forward to a new life. I was eager to get on with it, to get back to Lucy and James, and to face whatever had to be faced. I began to imagine changes – trivial, silly things. Perhaps I'd start by sorting out my wardrobe. I'd plan things better; get a dog; take more exercise.

Yes, I would experience a new sense of enjoyment. But it would be serious as well. I was as sure as anyone can be that there would be some public criticism of me for meeting Carlos. Somehow it didn't bother me. I would be able to handle it. I would have friends who would understand, my family would understand, and I would have a new sense of self-respect. All of this would carry me through. Even if nothing of the public Simon Weston were to remain, the private Simon Weston would be there, stronger than before.

I felt as if all these years I had been trapped inside a shell, a cocoon, and I was now ready to emerge into something new and fresh.

A bird screeched in the tree above me. I looked up. I had been on my own, in a sort of a trance, for almost two hours. In the distance, between the tree-trunks, I could see a truck on one of the dirt roads, sending up a cloud of dust.

Three men, the drivers of the cars and vans, were strolling towards me. One of them was sucking what looked like a silver tube which was stuck into a silver container. I wondered if this were some kind of drug. The one with the silver pot stuck his head into the van and held out the pot with a grin. It was filled with a slurry of green leaves, as though a very large plant-eating animal had just thrown up in it. Tea-break, South American style.

I took a tiny suck through the tube. Ugh. It had an acrid taste, like drinking cigarettes. I grimaced, making the men laugh, and handed the pot back.

The mood had been broken. I got out and wandered round. A hundred yards away, Gary and John were deep in conversation with the Argentinians, surrounded by the film crew. I noticed that the trees were part of a large garden that gave way to fields on either side. Along one side there was a tennis court.

I began to wonder if perhaps I was acting like a difficult child by not joining in. But no; no one over there would benefit from my presence. I was willing to do almost anything for a charity, or for the family, or friends, but there was no point my being there. Gary, John, and the Argentinians had all fought the war through to the end. I hadn't. They had things to talk about that I could not share. I would just destroy the purpose of the meeting, as well as possibly shattering my own sense of well-being. I strolled back to the van.

Malcolm came over, with the cameraman, Brian. 'What do you want to film me for?' I asked.

'I need it. So that people can make sense of why you are not at the meeting,' he replied.

Fine. I knew he wouldn't try to spring any surprises on me, and returned to my own inner peace and wandering thoughts. The family. My Mam. The need to make them all proud of me. The desire to put the last ten years behind me. I didn't have to keep reliving it, repeating those old patterns. If James was interested in what his dad had done, it was all there – on film and in print. I'd have moved on to other things: radio, perhaps; charity work; sponsorship; who knows what. 'Today is the first day of the rest of your life.' I liked that saying. Right then it really seemed like an important truth.

Just then a face appeared round the door of the van. It was Carlos.

As I learned later when I spoke to people who had talked to Carlos and Graciela during the filming, Carlos had been very puzzled by my absence, and perhaps just a little hurt.

He knew I was there, of course. He and Graciela had genuinely hoped I would be able to visit them in Mar del Plata, and were looking forward to seeing me again. He couldn't understand why I simply sat back there on my own. It was not the way he would have behaved. While the ex-soldiers talked over the campaigns, while the cameras rolled, he had been assuming that I would at least put in an appearance when people turned to the food and drink.

When I didn't appear, his vague sense of unease suddenly hardened into determination. He respected my decision. He knew that things were difficult for me – that much at least was explained to him – but, as he said later, he 'couldn't bear to see Simon sad'. He just wasn't going to let me get away with being so remote and stand-offish and, well, just plain British.

He felt the moment was right – he said it felt like 'the moment of take-off'. So, without even telling Graciela, he walked over to the van.

It was the first time we had been together alone, without an interpreter. I had picked up a couple of Spanish phrases, but neither '¡Manos arriba!' ('Hands up!') nor '¡Dos cervezas!' ('Two beers!') seemed very appropriate just at that moment. Carlos's English was very stilted. This didn't bother him. He was determined to give more of himself, and to get more from me, and he wasn't going to be put off by the small matter of language.

Slowly, painfully, he made me understand that he had left the Air Force, that he was working as a packaging salesman, that his children were a boy and girl, now aged fifteen and thirteen. Equally slowly, I told him about Lucy and the baby.

'The baby,' he said, 'is boy or girl?' Odd that we had talked for almost three hours the day before and hadn't exchanged many details of our children.

'Boy.'

'His name?'

'James.' Hadn't I told him that when we first met? I couldn't remember. I added that it was the name of one of my closest friends – my best man, Jimmy Salmon, who had helped save my life on the ship.

But I don't think he was listening. '*Increíble*,' he said. 'Name of *my* son is James – Santiago, Saint James.'

I stared at him. 'That's really strange,' I said.

Then for some reason, I suppose because other names are more important in his culture than mine, he asked: 'And the second name?'

'Andrew.'

His eyes widened further. 'Andrew,' he repeated. Then slowly, hesitantly: 'My daughter – the name of my daughter is Andrea.'

Now we were both staring and shaking our heads, almost lost for words. All I could say was 'Weird . . . freaky . . . incredible.' All he could say was: '*Increíble. Certamente.*'

There didn't seem much else we could say. What had been the chances of us choosing almost identical names for our children? Astronomical. Unless it wasn't chance, unless there was something else that connected us besides the bomb. This thought only made the coincidence seem even weirder.

Whatever it meant, I had to admit that Carlos's initiative had forged another link between us. It hadn't spoiled anything for me; and it had done something more for him. The sadness I had seen in his eyes two days earlier seemed to have gone, and I saw laughter there.

As we drove back an hour or so later, I thought: this time it's definitely over. I had done everything I had wanted to. I was free. No more Carlos. No more filming. For God's sake, it was time to move on, get to the Falklands, and get back home to Lucy and James.

Wrong again. Back at the hotel, to my surprise, there was Carlos, with a couple of the other Argentinians, sitting in the lobby. They were staying in town overnight. 'See you in the morning,' Carlos said cheerfully.

What was happening in the morning? Oh, yes; Gary, John and I were going to do a little more sightseeing. We had been having lunch in a café in Buenos Aires when Malcolm mentioned that the memorial to those Argentinians who died in the Falklands War was not far away. We said to each other, 'Oh, be nice to go along and have a look.' Not a big deal, just a brief, informal visit, just the three of us, so that we could pay our respects as private individuals.

However, unknown to me, another idea had emerged. The meeting at the ranch had gone well. Someone had let slip that the lads and I wanted to take a look at the memorial. Now the Argentinians were going to join us. Malcolm liked the idea. It would make another good sequence.

A personal meeting between myself and Carlos was all very well. A meeting between veterans on both sides was fine – ordinary blokes talking military matters informally without too much emotion. But this . . .

I imagined the three of us standing shoulder to shoulder with the other three in front of their equivalent of the Cenotaph, and the whole thing looking like an official statement that the war was over and the breach healed. I had a vision of Carlos and me being seen as symbols of peace and reconciliation. It seemed to me the whole thing would be well out of order, not just for me – John was out of the Army, but what would the Army families and the Army itself think of Gary? In his view, it would go down like a 'shit sandwich'.

Once again Malcolm reassured me. There would be no filming of us all together unless we were happy about it. No

Lucy and me on our wedding day, 12 May 1990.

With James, July 1991.

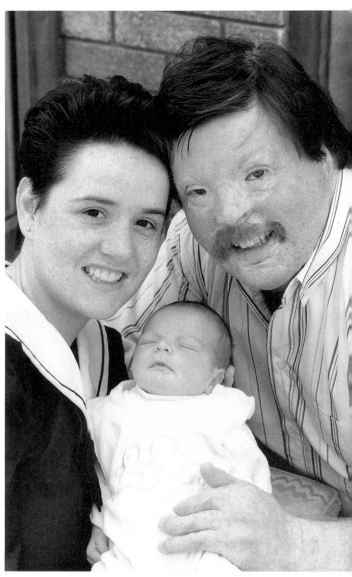

With Lucy and James, July 1991.

Meeting former Argentinian pilot Carlos Cachon in Buenos Aires, November 1991.

Carlos and his wife, Graciela.

Left to right: me, 58 Hughes, Yorkie and 11 Hughes, 1981. All three friends died in the fire on the *Sir Galahad*.

At the Stanley memorial which lists, among the dead, 58 Hughes, 11 Hughes and Yorkie.

he *Sir Galahad* shortly after the fire, June 1982.

t the Welsh Guards' memorial, Fitzroy, overlooking the bay where the *Sir
alahad* was hit.

With John and Gary at the Stanley memorial.

With Gary on Tumbledown.

With John – and a pair of Argentinian boots – on Wireless Ridge.

Stanley.

one would try to manipulate us into doing anything. Certainly there would be no suggestion that this was in any way official. It would be informal, discreet and personal. We would be in control.

OK. We decided we could live with that.

Next morning, off we went in the van to Juan Martín Square, a rolling expanse of well-tended grass dotted with trees. The day was cool and overcast, but the square was alive with parents, children and dogs.

At one end, set into the slope of a low hill, was the memorial, a curving wall of pink marble facing a flag-pole. Beyond the flag-pole was the road marking the end of the park, and after this a tall brick tower. It all looked quite new. Into the memorial wall were set twenty-five black plaques, with about twenty-five names on each: 'Those who fell in the struggle for the Malvinas and South Atlantic Islands'. There were 655 names there. This was the official number of Argentinian losses.

Our Argentinians were waiting for us: the veteran from Tumbledown, Carlos Vazquez; Juan Carlos Diez, who had been wounded on Wireless Ridge, and who claimed to have 'English blood' in him as the result of a transfusion in Stanley; Carlos Cachon, of course; and Ignacio Gorriti, an infantry company commander most of whose regiment had been captured at Goose Green.

And Juan Vallejos – a tall bloke with a moustache – who had also been on Wireless Ridge, but who was looking a bit out of place. I discovered why. It had been important to track down a man called Juan Vallejos, because, like Juan Carlos, he had been part of the only Argentinian counter-attack, just before they surrendered. He had been injured, had lost a leg, and now had a wooden one. The assistant producer and interpreter, Benetta, had gone through agonies, working through a maze of government departments, first to find Juan Vallejos – he was stationed somewhere on the other side of the country – then to get permission for him to be filmed, and then to make arrangements for him to fly to Buenos Aires. He had arrived on the morning of the meeting out at the ranch. Benetta had gone to pick him up. He came striding towards her. No wooden leg. By a weird coincidence, there had been two men named Juan Vallejos on Wireless Ridge. This was the wrong man. This one hadn't played an important part at all. Moreover, the poor guy had been so heavily warned not to say anything compromising that he was a bag of nerves – so scared he never really unwound.

While John did his best with his opposite number, Gary was soon deep in conversation with Carlos Vazquez. It was all quite informal, and the tension over filming vanished. It was also important, particularly because of Vazquez. Later I was to learn a good deal about him and what he had to say from Gary.

Vazquez, now a senior officer, had been a sub-lieutenant commanding a platoon on Tumbledown. He looked the image of the hard-bitten veteran – lean, short hair, moustache, muscular. But there was much more to him than this. He was also extremely emotional, most unusual for such a senior professional. He had reason. He was a man with a mission: to make sure that the truth was told about the Malvinas campaign.

He said the government had constantly sought to blame the Army for the defeat. Documentaries and articles always harped on about the inadequacy of the soldiers. No one looked at the politics of the defeat, the failure to look after the troops during the war, the lack of information, the terrible reception the men had when they returned. The truth was constantly covered up. Even the memorial itself – built only a couple of years earlier, right by a busy road, and set in full view of the 'English Tower', a building donated by the British government in the last century – was typical, he said, of the official but underhand campaign to denigrate the Army and cover up the impact of the defeat.

His main point concerned a tragic and disturbing subject: the 655 names on the memorial. 'But you know as well as me,' he said to Gary, 'that there were thousands of dead.'

Thousands. Gary was sure he said 'thousands'. To back up his point, Vazquez went through the names of those who had died in his platoon on Tumbledown: nine names – but he had lost seventeen. So he alone knew of eight men whose deaths had not been officially acknowledged.

Like a hidden sickness, the question of the Argentinian dead kept coming back – then and later. Almost half of the 655 were on the *Belgrano*, leaving only about 330 killed in the war itself. This didn't seem very many. Everyone 'knew' that many unrecorded Argentinian bodies were buried in trenches and dumped at sea. Perhaps there was a lot of rumour in the talk, because Argentinians have reasons to be suspicious of official statements concerning the war. But it was certainly well known that many bodies were never identified; and there were a lot of recent conscripts. It's easy in war to lose track of who's been sent where.

Carlos and Graciela were obviously pleased to see me again. And once more, despite my initial hesitation, I couldn't help warming to them, and greeted them like old friends. Soon Carlos was giving me much the same message as Vazquez was giving Gary. He also said he knew of ten dead whose names did not appear on the list. Did *every* survivor have a list of unrecorded victims? If so, the numbers could quickly add up to 'thousands'.

I wondered what all this meant for ordinary Argentinians. What must the families of those who died feel – especially those whose deaths went unrecorded – knowing their sons and brothers and fathers had fallen in a useless, hopeless gesture? And what of the survivors? The poor kids who fought there must have come back in humiliation, to a country that couldn't or wouldn't offer them the support they needed. I wondered what I would have felt if I had been rejected instead of looked after, and what the other two lads would have felt if they had been badly led doing a useless job – and lost? What sort of scars does all this leave on a country?

After looking round the memorial with Carlos, I described some of my own experiences in more detail. I mentioned the kids I saw on the *Canberra*, the youngest of whom was only thirteen, we were told. Carlos couldn't believe this, and I'm not sure I do, but the boy certainly looked no more than thirteen. I told him a little about the bomb, and how I got off the ship; my time in hospital; my recovery.

Then we moved on to less heavy subjects. Carlos told me severely I would really have to learn Spanish.

'Hey,' I said, 'I know some already: ¡*Dos cervezas!*'

'That's good,' Carlos laughed. 'You come again – and next time, you bring Lucy.'

'It's a deal.'

'But only if you promise to learn Spanish.'

'Well, I can't come back if I don't!'

'Right! Besides, you won't eat otherwise!'

Then, for a second time, Carlos hugged me goodbye. Pat Hill, the *News of the World* reporter, seized his chance and took the photo that later appeared on the front page of his paper. I wouldn't have chosen to embrace Carlos, certainly wouldn't have chosen that sort of exposure. But I knew Carlos now, I wasn't surprised, and the anger and confusion I had felt at our first meeting were things of the past. Something had shifted in me over those two days, thanks in part to Carlos himself. I can forgive myself for accepting his gesture. I hope the relatives of those who died at Carlos's hands can forgive as well.

Finally, one of the other Argentinians, Ignacio Gorriti, who spoke quite good English, handed me some dried flowers. 'I have a request,' he said. 'Would you place these in the British and Argentinian cemeteries in the Falklands?' I said I would be delighted. I had no problems about placing flowers on Argentinian graves. It would be an easy enough task, and it was only right to help them honour their dead. (He, too, mentioned that he knew of half a dozen names missing from the list of the dead.)

At the monument, a score of people had gathered to commemorate members of their families who had died in the war. It wasn't a regular event. Perhaps they had made a special journey together from a country area. They placed wreaths, then broke into an out-of-tune version of the Argentinian National Anthem, ending with a ragged cheer. It all seemed normal enough, but they were the lucky ones – they had the names up there to act as a focus for their grief.

What of the others – hundreds of families perhaps – whose sons' names were written nowhere, who could never come here, whose grief would never find a focus and a natural release?

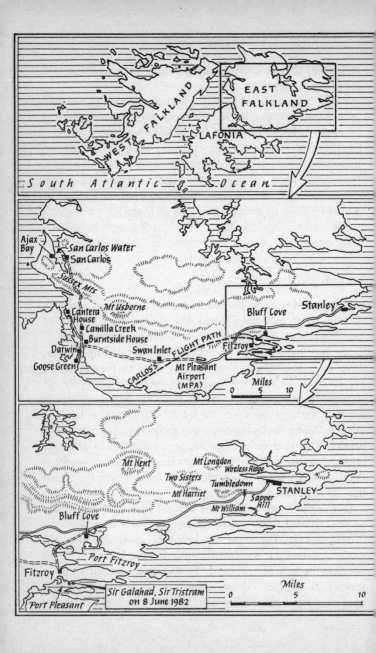

EAST
FALKLAND

WEST FALKLAND

LAFONIA

South Atlantic Ocean

Ajax Bay
San Carlos Water
San Carlos
Sussex Mts
Cantera House
Mt Usborne
Camilla Creek
Burntside House
Darwin
Swan Inlet
Goose Green
CARLOS'S FLIGHT PATH
Fitzroy
Bluff Cove
Stanley
Mt Pleasant Airport (MPA)

Miles
0   10

Mt Kent
Mt Longdon
Wireless Ridge
Two Sisters
Tumbledown
Mt Harriet
STANLEY
Sapper Hill
Mt William
Bluff Cove
Port Fitzroy
Fitzroy
Port Pleasant

Sir Galahad, Sir Tristram
on 8 June 1982

Miles
0   5   10

6

TO THE FALKLANDS

21–26 November 1991

It was a relief to leave Buenos Aires. It's a great city, but I've no plans to go back there. I had done what I came to do, and was eager to get on with the second half of the trip.

We were flying the long way round, via Chile. Before the war, there were direct flights from Buenos Aires to the Falklands, but not now. Air links, even non-government ones, are political statements, and there's a long way to go yet before either side is ready for that. So there we were, after a 600-mile jump over the Andes, dropping down to Santiago, with a few hours' break before the next leg of the journey southwards, into colder regions, almost to Cape Horn. From there, a small commercial flight, which makes the journey only twice a month, would take us back east to the Falklands.

Landing in Santiago took me straight back to Sicily, where we had landed when I was on my way to Kenya with the Welsh Guards. The same dry heat, the same dry hills, the grass scorched brown by the sun. I would have to look out for the top of my head. In this heat, I'd turn into a tomato in minutes. There seemed to be a strong military presence, from the planes and helicopters on the runways to the uniformed characters wtih machine-guns staffing the airport buildings.

This was an international flight, so we needed to clear customs. This brought an unexpected problem. Did I have anything to declare? Any food? Any fruit?

'No, only some dried flowers.'

That did it. The box containing the flowers for the British and Argentinian graves was opened. The man popped one of the dried seed pods, and shook his head. It was against regulations to bring the flowers in. Malcolm and Vanessa explained their purpose, but it did no good. The flowers had to go.

I was keen to take a look at the place, even if it was only for a couple of hours. Several of us took a cab from the airport and told the driver to run around town, then stop somewhere in the middle for a beer.

We found ourselves winding up a steep road up a mountain. The driver, who was beginning to be a fund of information, said he was taking us up to a virgin. I was beginning to think the Chileans were very hospitable people when I saw what he meant. On top of the mountain was a huge statue of the Virgin Mary. The road led to a couple of shops, and a few stalls where Indians sold carpets, ice-creams and mock swords made out of the 'swords' of swordfish. A radio was blaring out 'Who's crying now?' It was the sort of tourist trap you see the world over.

But the main feature of the place was its stunning view over the city. It lay in a plain between mountains, some of them snow-capped even in that heat. I was doing some videoing, and beginning to think I'd better find some shade, when I noticed the driver pointing. He was pointing at a stadium. I thought he was about to tell us something about the local football team, but no – this was the place where thousands had been killed under General Pinochet. 6,700 the driver said.

It was extraordinary. This sense of violence just below the surface seemed to be something typically South American.

During the next hour, as we flipped briefly around town, had a beer, and drove back out to the airport, we seemed to be in a stable, peaceful country. Yet only a year before it had been in the grip of a regime that had made thousands disappear, just as in Buenos Aires.

The driver said 50,000 had vanished in the country as a whole. He had friends who had been tortured and knew of families that had been destroyed when a son or daughter 'disappeared'. He said they had been taken into the countryside, shot and buried in trenches – killing fields that had still not been identified. Who had been involved? As far as I could gather, an intelligence service formed from four forces – the Police, the Air Force, the Army and the Marines. A year previously the reign of terror had come to an end; yet no one had been prosecuted. The killers were wandering around free.

The next leg of our journey was a longer one. Chile is a very strange shape – very long and thin, squashed between the high Andes and the coast. We'd already crossed the continent from east to west. Now we were heading 1,000 miles south, along the Andes.

Duncan, our assistant cameraman, looked down with a professional eye on the awesome snowy peaks below. He was a surprising bloke – wiry, with long curly hair down to his shoulders. Back in the Michelangelo in Buenos Aires, the waiter had called him 'Señorita'. Nothing effeminate about him, though – he was incredibly fit, and incredibly strong, because he is one of the best sports climbers in Britain, ranking in the top five. He worked as an assistant cameraman just to finance his climbing habit. We were flying over some of the most challenging climbs in the world. Like Mount Fitzroy: a peak battered by fearful weather, combining the most difficult aspects of both the Himalayas and the Alps. It had been climbed for the first time only in 1968. One day, Duncan would like to have a go.

Our stop-over was a windswept little town called Punta Arenas, set on the Straits of Magellan, which slice right across above Cape Horn, joining the Atlantic to the Pacific. Here, too, the military were everywhere: fighters, cargo planes, bunkers, dummy bunkers, helicopters, AA emplacements, rocket sites.

After checking in – the hotel was very good, better than the one in Buenos Aires – I took a walk with Gary down to the shore. It was a pretty miserable place, with an icy wind slicing up from the south. Two jets screamed low overhead, reviving memories of Argentinian planes on the Falklands. A huge high-sided cargo ship, perhaps an accommodation vessel for oil-workers, was manoeuvring slowly into dock. This was where the explorer Ferdinand Magellan had passed through on the first round-the-world voyage in 1520. No doubt it was better than going round the Horn, but someone (it turned out to be Duncan) had captured the spirit of the place by scrawling in the sand a huge arrow pointing south labelled 'Hell', and another pointing north labelled 'Home'.

We strolled up a hill, and looked around. I could see instantly why so many people had never been there. If I never saw the place again, it'd be too soon. To the north, the Andes run out. The hills are low, barren of anything except scrubby grass, and a few small wind-blasted trees and gorsebushes.

'Looks like the remains of a nuclear explosion,' I said.

'No,' Gary commented. 'It's not that nice.'

There is nothing much to the south – the other side of the straits – except lowlands stretching down to Cape Horn. After this, it's a stormy run down to Antarctica.

Below us, the town was a boring grid of streets; low buildings, lots of corrugated iron roofs painted blue, green and red. But it was a surprisingly active place. 150,000 people live there. The cars looked in better shape than they did in Buenos Aires, and the hotel was good, so there had to be some money about. Some of it must have come from the military. Chile and Argentina are not on the best of terms, and the land is divided oddly. Chile controls the Straits of Magellan, while Argentina has half of Tierra del Fuego. So the southern tip of Argentina is sliced off by Chile. They are still in dispute over a few islands on the cape. The town is also a main jumping-off point for expeditions to the Antarctic, especially for the Americans and British. And there is oil in the area, though I didn't see any obvious sign of it.

Next morning, we were off again in a twin-engined Otter. I'm a little nervous of small planes, after my experience trying for my pilot's licence, and there were things about this flight that made me wonder if we were going to make it. We'd just started to taxi when we came to an abrupt halt. A fire-engine roared out to meet us. No need to evacuate, though – the pilot had forgotten his passport.

We took off. The brown grass and distant grey hills dropped away as we headed north and east along the edge of the Magellan Straits. Below, cold waves broke on grey shores and a lone road cut across the drab landscape. In the distance, northwards, through rain that looked like a gauze, snow-capped mountains loomed briefly, and southwards harsh and treeless lowlands ran towards Cape Horn.

The landscape changed. A scattering of lakes appeared, looking like bomb craters. The sun broke through, splashing gold on the browns and greys. There wasn't a single house. A finger of land jutted out into the sea.

Suddenly the coast veered away northwards. We were over the southernmost part of Argentina now. Not much farther north was Río Gallegos, the base from which Carlos had taken off on his bombing missions. I could see blue-grey mudflats, grey sand, the brown of dry grass, and the green of shallow water. The colours swirled around each other like an abstract painting. Then we flew on into cloud, and South America dropped away behind us.

I settled back. My major concern was that ice was forming

on the wing-strut, just outside my window. Then, despite the 'No Smoking' sign, the loadmaster said it was OK for Gary to smoke. As he lit up, Duncan gently opened the door to the cockpit. There, in full view, was the spare fuel tank. Gary opened his eyes wide, and hurriedly put out his cigarette.

After this there were no further problems, at least not until we got there. I imagined that it would probably be an emotional experience, revisiting the places where my past was lost; but I had no idea what to expect, and so I had no reason to anticipate. I had not read much about the war, and certainly never read anything about the Falklands. I felt drained of emotion, waiting for whatever was coming next.

Now we were dropping slowly down through the clouds. The first bit of the Falklands appeared – a flat, grey streak, hardly rising above the water. Then more small islands, and a coastline with inlets and peninsulas. Beneath the clouds, through flurries of rain and patches of mist, I saw a drab, treeless expanse of moorland. We had come 8,000 miles to fight for *this*? It was hard to understand, as crazy as if Argentina had decided to send a task force to the Shetlands.

Another stretch of water. A rocky coastline, sand dunes covered with rough grass, then more of the camouflage colours of the grass and peat landscape. Perhaps we had just crossed the Falkland Sound that divided East and West Falklands. We must have flown close by the place where I had first come ashore. I could see tracks across peat, peat cuttings, a few sheep.

Then suddenly, a line of houses, Nissen huts, some trailer homes, all scattered along the edge of a large inlet. It looked like a village on a Scottish sea loch.

We banked. Below was a wreck. For a moment I wondered if it was left over from the war. No – it was much older, a rusty hulk, perhaps from the late nineteenth century. Then a muddy chaos of building works. We swung into land – and there, right in front of us was a communications mast. The engine revved. We rose, sank again, and landed.

A small white building, blanketed in rain, announced 'Stanley Airport'.

We climbed down into driving rain, directed by weather-beaten men in waterproof clothing. They wouldn't have looked out of place on a North Sea trawler. Someone pointed out a cable dangling from the tail-plane. Was that the Otter's radio aerial? Or had we picked it up from the mast behind us? God, every time I came here something nasty seemed to happen.

'Bloody weather you brought with you!' said a bearded figure with a grin, recognizing me. It was good to hear an English voice again, after all that Spanish.

'Not much different from the last time I was here,' I replied.

'Well, it must be you that brought it, then.'

We hurried into the little white house to find ourselves going through customs, of all things. It seemed odd to be arriving on an international flight at such a small place.

Then on, in four-wheel-drive vehicles, into Stanley, with our driver Tony, a softly-spoken bloke of about thirty. We had landed close by the town, in the old terminal. A new RAF and Army base, built up since the war, was situated about thirty-five miles away. This provides the only direct air link with Britain.

God, what a miserable arrival: rain, bitter wind, flurries of sleet, even a quick hailstorm. In the first few hours we seemed to get a dose of the worst of British weather. And this with summer around the corner. John and Gary assured me that it could change equally quickly for the better, but I hardly dared believe them. All I could remember – from that wet and windy trip on the *Galahad* ten years earlier – was the grimness.

At first glance, Stanley didn't offer much to lift the spirits. It's situated on a rise that skirts Stanley Harbour, an estuary five miles long and about half a mile across. It really is a small place, no more than a village, with around 2,000 people mainly living in wooden prefab houses imported from Britain. There are four pubs, two hotel bars, a disco, no cinema, a supermarket, and a few smaller shops, all stocked with basic corner-shop goods, and that's about it. You can hire videos, but there isn't much else to do with your spare time.

Mostly it has the feel of a 1950s suburb, with the houses crowded together – odd when you think of all the space round about. There are a few lines of terraced houses straight out of the 1930s. Some new houses were being built, in more modern designs, so I supposed the population was growing.

The grandest house is the governor's – a graceful Victorian building defended against the everlasting wind by evergreens. Apparently it takes a good deal of tender loving care to grow trees there. There are a few in Stanley, one at the other end of the estuary, and that's about it. I didn't see any others anywhere.

It was odd to come half way round the world and arrive at a place looking like a slice of Scotland, with bacon, sausages and eggs for breakfast. This was welcome, and I was sure I would get on with the people, but I couldn't imagine I'd be able to generate much affection for the landscape or the town. Still, I didn't want to make up my mind yet – the fact that people chose to settle here must mean that it had something going for it.

We were staying in two hotels, a larger one, the Upland Goose – named after one of the island's best known birds – and a little place converted from a private house, Emma's.

Both gave a view over the estuary. A grassy bank guarded by a couple of ancient cannons looked across the inlet to a range of low hills forming part of Wireless Ridge. The slopes were covered in yellow-brown patches of grass broken by grey stone that burst through to make a rocky spine. Lower down, smaller stones had been made into huge grey letters that picked out the names of ships – *Barracuta, Beagle, Protector, Endurance* – the Royal Naval vessels assigned to the area over the last century. (Darwin had come here in a ship called *Beagle* on his round-the-world voyage in 1834, but this was a different one.)

Away to the left, if the weather was clear, you could see the sharp cone of Mount Kent and the lower, ragged heights of Tumbledown – names from a past I was close to, but never a part of. This time around, I would be.

As we were stuck in Stanley for a day or two, the first thing I wanted to do was to check up on the only contact I had in the Falklands – Ann Green. Her son Paul had been in the Guards with me, and was one of those killed in the *Galahad* fire. I knew Ann had moved down to the Falklands after the war, and thought I might be able to persuade her to put on a kettle for me, if I could find her.

It didn't take long. Tony knew her, because she lived two doors down from him, a short windy walk from the hotel. I strolled round to find her. The house, a couple of hundred yards up the slope from the shore, looked like a seaside boarding house, with a glassed-in verandah, except that it had a corrugated iron roof. It overlooked a kids' playground and a few Nissen huts and garages.

When I knocked on her door, it was just on the off-chance of finding her in. But there she was, delighted to see me, and more than happy to make a brew. We had met briefly at a service in St Paul's Cathedral in 1985, at the dedication of a war memorial.

Pretty soon we were deep into our memories, looking through Ann's photographs with her daughter, Carol: Irish Guards trooping the colour one hot summer's day around 1980 – I could remember watching it from the street; my squad training – old friends, far-off times; Windy Miller, who took a burst of shrapnel in the face in Northern Ireland; Maxy MacDonald, one of my instructors; and, of course, Paul himself, looking as rough as I remembered him.

Ann had had five kids in all – the oldest, Carol, then two boys, Paul and Michael, then twins. Paul could be a pretty difficult character, not to say violent, as Ann will admit. I never knew why until then.

He'd been badly burned when he was three, and as a kid he always wore long shorts to cover his scarred thighs. Later, there had been emotional fits, suicide attempts, psychiatrists' reports, and small-time trouble with the Police until he joined the Welsh Guards. When I knew him, he was still trouble, but by all accounts he was a lot quieter than he had been. Ann said he loved every minute of the Guards, enough to inspire his brother Michael to join as well, with tales of regular money, and drinks, and loads of girls.

She had seen him and Michael off on the *QE2* on 12 May, with the sun shining and the bands playing and everyone cheering and crying. 'I couldn't take my eyes off Paul,' she said, 'Michael was standing right beside him, but all my vision was full of Paul's face. I had this feeling then that this was the last time I was going to see him again.'

'Yes,' Carol added. 'Michael always used to say, "Don't worry about me. I've got a return ticket." But with Paul it was, "What will be, will be."'

When Carlos made his approach, Paul was playing cards down on the tank deck, a few feet away from me as I was making for Yorkie. One of Paul's friends – who later told Ann what happened – had just appeared to find him, telling him there were some blue movies being shown upstairs in Accommodation.

'I'll be up when I've finished this hand,' Paul said.

Just about then, the alarm call came, and I squatted down on the deck, and Carlos's bomb came across in front of me. Paul must have been almost as close as I was to the explosion, but why he should have died while I lived I have no idea.

Back home, Carol was in the middle of her engagement party when she saw a little black car pull up outside the house, and an official-looking man get out. She knew at once.

'I've some bad news,' he said, at the door.

'It's Paul, isn't it?'

Yes. He had been reported missing, but Carol and Ann were

certain of the truth, even before the message came through the next day: 'Presumed dead'.

Yet, despite the despair inside her, Carol kept on with the party. Paul had paid for half of it, and a small voice inside her said: if he comes back and finds I've cancelled the party, he'll call me a silly cow and give me a clip round the head.

A year later, in May 1983, Ann was on the Ministry of Defence trip to the Falklands for families of the dead. She was still deep in grief for Paul, and you would have thought she'd have felt nothing but bitterness. Far from it – she fell in love with the place. She loved the peace, the silence, the wildness, the cleanness, the safety, the freedom from the stresses of life back home. She loved the people – two jumbo jets filled with relatives arrived in Stanley, yet everyone was made welcome in someone's home. She was overwhelmed by the generosity, the gratitude and the sympathy.

When she visited San Carlos – where the first landings had taken place – it was a beautiful day, and the hills that looked so drab when it rained were golden in the sunlight. It was certainly not the grim, wet and icy lump of moorland the press had depicted. A thought came to her: if this place is worth dying for, it's worth living for.

As soon as she got home she decided she would like to emigrate. Her friends were shocked. They told her she was sick, she only wanted to be near Paul, she should face reality, and anyway the Falklands was a lump of rock in the middle of nowhere. She knew better on all counts, and the family backed her. A letter to the Falklands landed her a job as cook in the Upland Goose Hotel. By November she was on her way. She'd never regretted it.

It was strange how Paul's death had changed Ann's life – and Carol's. She was an announcer on the local radio, something she would never have done if she'd stayed at home. Ann looked as if she had come through some rough times, but I'm sure she had made the right move.

Hers was a story that made me think there might be a bit more to the islands than met the eye.

That evening, me and the lads found a local, Deano's. It was home from home – noisy, crowded with young people – mostly construction workers and squaddies in jeans and T-shirts – hazy with smoke and beer. I don't indulge all that much now, but there was nothing else on offer in Stanley, and it was good to have a few ales with Gary and John.

Besides, I got a pretty good reception. Several people recognized me, so we weren't short of company. A DJ told me all about the local karaoke evening – we attended one later, and it was a trial, with the same performers doing the same songs week after week. One young lady wanted to have her picture taken with me, together with her friend; but her friend was so shy she could hardly speak, let alone get into the picture. It took all my powers of persuasion to get her to stand beside me, to look up and smile. By the time we were done, she seemed happy, which made me happy for her.

The noisy conversation also gave me a chance to learn a little more about the place. One piece of gossip was interesting. Apparently everyone here, too, 'knew' that many more Argentinians had been killed than their government would admit to. There were stories of Argentinian troops burning bodies on a headland near Stanley and dumping bodies at sea. This was another reason for taking seriously all that talk about thousands of Argentinian dead unaccounted for.

Deano's attracted some pretty odd characters – and some surprising ones. One was the harbour owner, with a neck thicker than mine, carpet-beater hands, and eyes that looked as though he'd been on a three-week piss-up. Another had a ring in one ear and low eyebrows. His name was Paul – Paul 'Scouse' they called him, because he was from Liverpool. His story was one laugh after another.

He might have looked rough, but he was a military policeman.

He was in the Falklands as a punishment. As a *punishment*? For what? For being drunk and disorderly and conspiring to assault. It transpired that he had been out on the town with a mate when the mate was picked up by the local police. Then they picked on Paul, simply because he was in the area. Paul kept quiet about his occupation. At four in the morning, he called his solicitor. They sued for wrongful arrest. Politically this was not a good move – not good for relations between the military and the civilian police. So he was posted to the Falklands to keep him out of harm's way.

No sooner was he down here than he heard he'd won his case. He was richer by two grand. More than that – he *loved* it. This coarse-looking, ear-ringed street-fighter type had fallen in love with the wild life. He was mad keen on photography. He chattered away like an even rougher version of David Bellamy about white-sand beaches, and nesting penguins, and killer whales, and pregnant dolphins, and the red-banded caracara – whatever that is. He was involved with a girlfriend, and had just requested that his punishment posting be doubled.

Work? Not too much of that. He had seven cases in four months, all of them civilian, except for one. He'd found a private asleep on guard duty out at the Mount Pleasant base. There were rockets, vehicles, God knows what in the compound. Some drunk might have sneaked in and driven off with a Rapier.

How much was all this stuff worth, anyway?

'120 million pounds, Corporal.'

What?!

Paul's face registered genuine horror. He'd recommended a court martial.

It was partly because of Paul that I went on my first trip outside Stanley. Tony took me out past the wreck we had seen from the plane – a rusty hulk that the SAS had hidden in for a couple of weeks to spy on the Argentinians in Stanley – to a beach called

Gypsy Cove. It was a delightful spot, with sands as white as the Caribbean, deserted (of course) and sheltered. Offshore lay the ominous dark strands of the huge, rubbery kelp that gives the islanders their nickname – 'Kelpers'.

The only Falklanders around, though, were the birds, mainly upland geese and penguins. The penguins, very smart and dignified, paraded into the shallows, surged about like seals, and stared out of their burrows, cocking their heads from side to side as if they couldn't believe their eyes. They acted as if they had never been disturbed in their lives.

There may not have been much in the way of entertainment in town, but at least we had the wit and wisdom of the photographer, David Thorpe, who had joined us in Stanley. David was a delightful character – professional, yet never intrusive or demanding, and also very funny. I could do with all the laughs I could get.

He was not, at first sight, someone with film-star qualities. Let's say he was no longer in the first flush of youth. Not too tall. Like me, he didn't suffer from a flat stomach. No denying his charm, though – easy to talk to, a fund of anecdotes from a varied life, and an obvious delight in his family. We were chatting over supper at the Upland Goose, and I said how nice it must be to travel so much – the people, the women . . .

He surprised me by saying that, yes, travel always restored his faith in his own sexual prowess.

And him a family man. Oh, dear.

He caught my eye. 'Let me tell you about Dr Feinstein's Law of Sexual Polarity,' he said, and began to explain, in a street-wise London voice so deadpan it took a while for me to catch on.

'Wonderful thing, the unconscious.' His tone was slightly superior, as if he was telling me something I really ought to know. 'If anyone enters the room, you're unconsciously aware. Beautiful woman comes in. Before you know it, you check her out. It's an automatic response. Stands to reason.'

I nodded. I couldn't think what he was getting at. He carried on.

'It's the same when a man goes into a room. The women notice. But with women it's different. They guard their reactions, don't they? With me, though, the effect is really dramatic. When I go into a bar in a hotel abroad, I'm on expenses, the places are pretty good, inevitably there are one or two beautiful women there. Inevitably, something very extraordinary happens. *Not one of them looks at me!*'

I gave him a sympathetic smile. Now we were getting to the sob stuff. Middle age creeping on, no longer attractive to women etc.

He took a sip of wine. 'At first when this happened, I was hurt, because I thought they hadn't noticed me. But that didn't make sense. Of course they'd noticed me. Of course I had registered in their subconscious. So why didn't they look at me? Was it because I wasn't worth looking at?

'No. Deep down. I knew that was ridiculous. I mean, there would be a reaction sometimes, wouldn't there? Law of averages. Then I realized what was really going on. *I was too attractive for them*! The impact of my personality, my looks, my animal sexuality – it was all too much. They knew that if they once looked up, if our eyes once met, they would be lost. At my feet. Their world in ruins.

'There was only one possible response: they had to pretend to ignore me. It was the only way they could avoid becoming my complete slaves.

'Of course, it's all done at the unconscious level. If you tried to get them to admit the truth – I'd never do it, because it would be cruelty, wouldn't it? – but if you tried, they would deny it. Well, they'd have to, wouldn't they? You can laugh,' he added, seriously, 'but it's quite true.'

'And now I know the truth, it's a great source of strength.

Every time I go into a foreign bar, and the women all ignore me, I know what's going on inside them, and I feel this warm glow of male pride.

'I could have any woman I want, any time. But it's better this way. I like to see proof that I'm getting more attractive with every passing year.'

He drained his glass, and pushed back his chair. 'That's why I love foreign travel. It's a continual boost to the ego. Wonderful thing, the unconscious. 'Night.'

Slowly, I was beginning to get an inkling of what the Falklands were all about.

Before the war, the Argentinians had been on their way to taking over the place. The British government hadn't really been interested. The Argentinians had the air link, they were the obvious trading partner, and they had put some cash into the islands' economy. The islanders had no alternative but to respond. Many people told me that if Argentina had continued to play it cool, it would have been given the place within a few years.

As it was, Galtieri simply shot himself in the foot. The islanders had always considered themselves to be as British as me. Whatever the official attitude, they were legally British. We had no choice but to respond. After this, there was no way that Britain could be seen to be betraying the islanders.

As a result, the islands had never been so secure. There had been only forty marines there in 1982; now there were almost 2,000 troops, a huge base and a growing economy. The governor had just opened up the islands for oil exploration. This would lead to a mini-boom. Soon there would be more people, more houses and more jobs.

Was this good or bad? I had no idea yet, but I was beginning to look forward to finding out.

It might not be a place I would choose to live in, but it promised to be a more interesting one than I had imagined.

7

SAN CARLOS

26–27 November 1991

I had always said the first place I wanted to visit was San Carlos, because that was the first place I came ashore – well, the only place that I remember anything about. I knew there was a memorial there – probably nothing much more than a cross and a few words on a headstone – but I didn't expect the visit to be all that emotional, because nothing much had happened there for me. It would be an easy way to start re-experiencing the past.

The night before, over an ale or three, somebody had asked what I was doing next.

'Going to San Carlos.'

'Oh, going camp, are you?'

I gave him a look. Was he looking for a slap in the gob, or what? Damned cheek. I didn't think I had been acting particularly effeminately. But no – it transpired that all areas outside Stanley are referred to as the 'camp', short for the Spanish *campo* ('field' or 'countryside'). Well, all right. Yes, I was going camp.

San Carlos lay on the other side of East Falkland, only sixty-five miles away, and half of that was paved now. But according to Tony, our main driver, the last few miles were a rough ride over moors and mountains. This last section might take three hours or more, depending on whether we bogged down or not. There are Welsh Guards who could probably beat a Land Rover over the same course.

We headed out in a convoy of three four-wheel drive vehicles. Two of these were modern long-wheel-base machines with bulbous tyres; one was older, with a short wheel-base and an unorthodox solution to the problem of peat and mud – its owner, Tony, had welded another set of wheels on to the back wheels. This one was being driven by Gary.

There was even a minor challenge about the first few miles, out to the RAF and Army base at Mount Pleasant Airport, or MPA as it's called. The road leading west between mountains and the coast was mostly gravel. It was solidly made, with a good curved surface to provide run-off for the rain. But the combination of slippery gravel and a sloping surface made the going a little dicey, especially as the engineers had dug huge six-foot ditches on either side. It felt more like navigation than driving.

On several occasions we skirted mine-fields. The Argentinians had laid tens of thousands of mines, some on the west coast, but most around Stanley. There were many types, from small three-inch anti-personnel mines to anti-tank mines; so many that it would take years and millions of pounds to clear them. The engineers had done their best, and then simply fenced off the rest. Maps are easily available from the Royal Engineers HQ in Stanley, where the types of mines found are on display.

There are 115 marked mine-fields, many contained within miles of fenced-off areas that are marked on the map in red – 'known to be still mined'. They look large when you see them, but in fact they can be measured in acres rather than square miles. Along parts of the coast, explosive devices have occasionally been found washed up by the tide. The Engineers are careful – *all* the remainder of the islands are marked blue, which means 'may still contain unexploded bombs, ammunition, missiles etc.' Very few areas are marked green, meaning they've been 'exhaustively checked', which is as good as saying they're guaranteed clear. In fact, I don't think there has been a single mine-related incident since the war. It's quite a record.

If you knew nothing about mines, you might think that the peace might occasionally be shattered by an exploding penguin, but in fact it takes a certain pressure to detonate even the most sensitive anti-personnel mine. I saw the carcass of a sheep in one mine-field, but I think it had died of boredom. The penguins and seals are certainly safe.

Anyway, there we were, driving on ball-bearings above six-foot ditches past mine-fields, in a fog of dust thrown up by the car in front.

Every now and then we were threatened by death-defying sheep. They are as silly on the Falklands as anywhere else. They see you coming and start running away ahead of you. The car catches up, the sheep panic and decide just as you draw level that it's safer on the other side of the road – and cut straight across in front of you.

Dust, slippery gravel, sloping roads, six-foot ditches, kamikaze mutton and mine-fields: God help the Argentinians if they ever try a quick run in from MPA.

We were heading west, across the gentle lower slopes of mountains that were familiar from the war: William, Harriet, Challenger. The flanks of the hills were camouflage colours – patches of dark green heather and lighter green and brown grass, all flowing down from the light grey spines of rock. These were the same colours that had depressed me when I first saw them from the plane, but the day was clear, and the air so clean that distant summits stood out as sharp as nearby rocks, and the sun and clouds scattered patches of shadow and light. Perhaps it wasn't quite so grim as I had first thought.

It might have been a part of Scotland, except for something that I had never seen before. Not surprisingly, as it turned out, because it, or rather they, are special to the Falklands. Now and then, the grassy slopes on either side of the road were divided by odd outcrops of rock. After we had passed several, I recognized them as the 'rivers of rock' that I'd heard someone mention in Deano's. Now I remembered – we'd been told about them when we were coming south on the *QE2*: watch out for the rocks; you could break a leg on them if you try to walk over them, and there are sometimes huge drops down into God knows what.

They were puzzling things. The rocks all seemed to be good-sized boulders, all within a certain range of sizes, none of them small enough to lift by hand, and none much larger than a car. They were mostly lying in channels, like rivers that seemed to be leading down from the bare upper slopes. But sometimes they spread out into little plains, like rock lakes. Some seemed to have been lying there dead for thousands of years, and were covered all over with heather and grass. But others were uncovered, as if they were still moving.

As an ex-soldier my first thought was: bloody awful ground to fight over. Somewhere to our right was Tumbledown. Imagine crawling over thirty yards of this rubble, on a freezing night, carrying a rifle with bayonet attached, trying to keep quiet, when every move makes a scrape and a clang, and there are enemy trenches ahead, and flares above and snipers up on the higher ridges.

But I couldn't help wondering about how they had been formed, these 'rock runs', because you see them on all the hillsides. I had never bothered about geology, so I guessed that they must have been made by ice – perhaps by Ice Age glaciers. Perhaps in winter this was where ice formed, and where water flowed in spring. But nothing seemed to make much sense, and no one I met knew the answer. And why aren't there rock runs anywhere else – in the Brecon Beacons or in Scotland?

Over to the left, towards the sea, there were three or four houses, the first signs of life outside Stanley. Bluff Cove, home to perhaps a dozen people. Beyond lay Fitzroy, and the inlet where the *Galahad* had moored. Well, time enough for that later.

On, through dust, across white tussocky grasslands, towards MPA. In all those thirty-five miles there was just one roadside building, a hotel, of all things, presumably catering for civilians who came in on the RAF flight and wanted a real taste of the wilds before hitting the dizzy metropolis of Stanley.

MPA itself was an eye-opener – we stopped there to buy some dried flowers for the memorials, replacements for those taken by the Chilean customs. The place was a square mile of runways, hangars, offices, shops and living quarters, all neat greens and whites, with tarmacked roads, each named with solid British signs in solid black British typeface. One of our few overseas outposts – and a new one at that. A self-contained world for 2,000 people.

What was it all for? Simply to make sure the Argentinians didn't think of trying it again? Or was it all part of a longer term, strategic plan, to do with future investments, oil and minerals, and defending British interests in Antarctica and South America? Perhaps, after the war, men in dark suits had let their minds wander to what might happen if we were to find oil there, and the Russians got nasty or South America really went down the tubes. Perhaps they had had words with their pals in Washington. It might be useful for us and the North Americans to have a big, secure base in the South Atlantic. Perhaps, also, it might be useful to have huge expanses of harsh landscape for training in. Perhaps a lot of things. One thing was for sure: no one was going to pull out of there in a hurry.

After this the road turned into a track. It had been a track for many years, but just then it was hard going, because a new road was being built across the peat and grass. In a year or so the run to Goose Green would be a doddle. But right then it was an obstacle course. We slalomed around bulldozers and scrapers and piles of gravel and top-soil. We accelerated briefly along newly scraped mud. We crawled over untouched peat. We hopped in and out of the vehicles to open and shut sheep-gates. The rough pasture stretched away unbroken on either side. We had swung away from the mountains – they now ran far to the right, over five miles away, not that you could judge distance in that sparkling air.

There was something else about the plant life here, now that I saw it close up. The surface was covered with plants I had never seen before. Known as 'balsam bogs', they consisted of thin twigs densely matted into pin-cushion shapes. They looked like giant puff-balls. They were quite solid, but not solid enough to support you, and certainly not solid enough to offer resistance to a Land Rover's wheel.

Twenty miles and a couple of hours later, Tony led us down off the peat on to hard sand, because it was an easier route when the tide was out. The coast stretched away to the left. We could see a collection of white-painted houses, with red and green corrugated iron roofs. Then up, with the ribbed wheels taking a good grip of the soft soil, and on to a ridge.

We were on a land bridge, a mile wide and five miles long – a strip of land that prevents East Falkland being sliced in two. To the south, the island opens out again into its other half, Lafonia.

On the land bridge itself stood two little settlements: Darwin and Goose Green – the houses we had seen further back. This was familiar territory to John; it was the scene of his first battle, and the first big one of the war. But this wasn't our destination yet. We were heading on around the coast, northwards, beyond the end of the road, up over the Sussex Mountains, to San Carlos.

Now we were really getting into the wilds. The convoy of three vehicles forded a stream, axle-deep. John remembered wading through it when he led his platoon towards Goose Green. He had good cause to remember it. It had been night, and very cold. Already his feet were wet, and now he had to get a lot wetter. 'As I crossed I could feel I was slipping deeper, deeper, deeper. Aaah! Don't let me get wet nuts! Too late. I was expecting two little frozen lumps to appear out the top of my collar.'

We headed uphill over the thick cushion of peaty soil. Although San Carlos had been occupied for a century – every now and then we saw the course of an old wagon-track – no one had pioneered a track for motor-driven vehicles. Each driver was a pioneer, searching out his own course. It was no good following someone else – the wheels often cut through the surface ploughing up mud that was best avoided by anyone coming after.

It required a strange kind of skill, heading steadily uphill over the broad tussock-covered flanks, swinging the wheel back and forth to avoid soft spots and outcrops of rock and small ponds of black, peaty water. Often it was impossible to see why Tony chose one direction over another. There seemed to be no difference between this yellow patch of grass and that.

Our lads were good, but they didn't make a big deal of it. Sometimes locals did the same run in the dark, when things could really get tricky. 'You think you know every blade of grass until something goes wrong,' the hotel-owner in San Carlos told me after we arrived. She had been stuck coming this same route a few days earlier, until an SOS call on the radio summoned help from San Carlos. It took a few hours, but another vehicle, with a winch, sorted her out.

Not many cars came this way, perhaps half a dozen a week, but this was enough to show how fragile the wilderness was. There were tyre-marks from weeks, even months, earlier. The old wagon-track was a permanent scar, with no signs of growing over. If more cars came, the whole mountainside would become a churned-up mass of peaty mud that would never be allowed to heal. One day, there would have to be a road. Then what? More settlers, and an end to a century of isolation?

This was the land John had advanced over ten years earlier.

We stopped briefly at one site he remembered, Camilla Creek. Back then it was a house. Now the house had gone. There was nothing but some bits of concrete and a few poles, the wind that whipped away your words as you spoke and clouds blanketing the summits of the hills.

We began to weave along the spine of the Sussex Mountains. The views became ever grander, though clouds were now lowering over the high ground. I still wouldn't have called it beautiful, because it's not my sort of landscape, but it was definitely spectacular. Below, the tongues of land licked round inlets and lagoons. The sea was untroubled by the gusting wind, perhaps because it was protected by the shores of West Falkland, easily visible less than ten miles away.

Further along the ridge, San Carlos Water came into view below us, a grey mirror of sea reflecting a grey sky. The bank of mountains ran on and curved behind the inlet like a protective arm. Somewhere on the lower slopes – invisible – was Ajax Bay, where I was taken after I was injured.

We stopped again. John had spotted another of his sites – a shallow trench with stone and peat walls. This miserable shelter had been his home for two or three days at the beginning of the war.

Like everyone else, they had made the mistake of digging in. This was when they discovered that the peat was like a sponge – it oozed. Dig down, and what you had was not a cosy protection but an ice-bucket half full of water. That was when the lads started getting trouble with trench-foot. No one ever found a decent solution. When you set up a new position, you had to dig in immediately, just to be sure of some sort of protection. But as soon as you could, the thing to do was build *up*, make thick wind-proof walls of peat turf and put a cape over the top. Then, if you could get dry, you could remain snug for hours. All around were the results, still visible ten years on.

We eased on down to San Carlos. I had spent eight days in the area, but my memories were all of carrying packs, brewing tea, cold feet and miserable nights, the long hike up the Sussex Mountains, and back down again when the powers that be decided we wouldn't make it on foot.

I recognized the jetty where we had landed, and the white house with the red-painted roof near which we had had our horrible exposed latrine. I remembered the trench I had shared with Colin Parsons. I even found it before we left San Carlos the next day, up under a ridge, close to a bridge. Still there after ten years! Well, not so much a trench, hardly more than a shell-scrape – just enough to get a bit of shelter in case of a bombing raid. But by then we knew there were no enemy soldiers around, and the thick clouds meant no chance of bombs, so we felt safe enough to brew up. All around, in the bitter night, stoves flickered.

The countryside looked much as I remembered it, though I'm sure it was nicer then. There had been a mud slide in the ridge above the little scrape. You could see the ripples in the side of the hill. Another ten years, and the scrape will have vanished, so if anyone wants to do any archaeological research at this extremely important site, they better get a move on.

The settlement itself, which I had never seen much of ten years earlier, looked surprisingly civilized. Good green grass, not the straggly pale yellow stuff of the slopes above. Three houses with red, green and blue roofs of corrugated iron. Hedges glowing with yellow gorse flowers. One of the houses was the Blue Beach Hotel, where we were staying, but this wasn't our first objective.

First came the memorial. We parked, unloaded, and followed one of the locals right on past the hotel, past a second house, along a track lined with gorse, through a gate, and into a field that sloped down to the sea.

I hadn't any idea what to expect, so I was taken totally by surprise, both by the sight, and by the sudden rush of emotion.

Ahead of me as I walked down the field, with its neat

wooden fence, was a little inlet of San Carlos Water. This was Blue Beach where the first troops – 'A' Company of 40 Commando – waded ashore from their landing craft early in the morning of 21 May. Offshore, in the darkness, waited the two assault ships *Fearless* and *Intrepid*. As the sixteen landing craft, with their 1,200 troops, chugged towards the shore, no one knew what to expect. There was a quick, intense fire-fight going on to the left, as Special Boat Services cleared about 100 Argentinians up on Fanning Head, which guarded the entrance to San Carlos Water. Intelligence reports said there weren't any Argentinian troops at San Carlos itself. And there had been lots of diversionary raids – one of them on Darwin, on the other side of the Sussex Mountains – to confuse the enemy about our intentions. But Intelligence might be wrong, and the Argentinians might not have been fooled. Perhaps it would be like the Normandy invasion: enemy planes, bombs, bullets, mine-fields, the lot.

As it happened, there was no one there. Total silence.

Men of 40 Commando had walked up the same track to the manager's house behind me, to ask the manager, Pat Short, if there were any Argentinians about. Pat is still there, in the same house. He told the story later. John Thurman, who had visited San Carlos a few months earlier, was told to knock on the door, so that at least Pat was confronted by a familiar face. Pat, the first Falklander to be liberated, seemed not at all surprised to see men armed to the teeth, their faces blacked for night combat.

'Hello, Pat,' said John. 'Do you remember me?'

Pat peered into the darkness at the shadowy figures with their camouflaged faces.

'Are you . . . British?' he asked, warily.

'Yes. It's John. John Thurman.'

'Oh, you've come then,' said Pat. Not over-emotional, the Falklanders. A Commando who was there later said he was sure that 'if we had been grass-skirted Chinamen with daggers in our teeth, the reception would have been the same'.

At the top of the field, just where the first position had been established, was the memorial. It was then I began to feel I was in the presence of something special, and the feeling grew as I approached.

The setting was truly beautiful. A five-foot wall of light-coloured, yellow Falklands stone had been built in a circle, with a gate facing downhill, towards the inlet. The two arms of the inlet swung out to sea on either side. Across the bay, the great grey bank of the Sussex Mountains loomed, their upper slopes shrouded in mist.

Behind the memorial circle stood a Union Jack fluttering from a flag-pole, and behind the flag-pole there was a huge bank of gorse, bright with yellow flowers. The only sounds were the gusts of wind, the cries of sea-birds, and the steady slap-slap-slap of the flag-pole rope.

But it wasn't the setting that really got to me. It was what I saw when I walked through the gate. I was in a small cemetery – beautifully trimmed lawn, a few graves, and a flower-bed of daffodils tucked in under the wall, protected from the wind and cold. At the far end, the stone wall rose to form a higher section about ten feet high holding dark marble plaques. I went straight up to it to see exactly what they said.

Words engraved in the marble paid tribute to the Task Force, but in particular 'to the abiding memory of the sailors, soldiers and airmen who gave their lives and who have no grave but the sea. Here beside the graves of their comrades this memorial records their names.'

I was totally unprepared for the effect these words had on me. 'Those who have no grave but the sea.' That could have been me. I stood there, with tears in my eyes, utterly destroyed by the emotion.

I scanned the names. Many of them were familiar: Ian Anthony Dale and Brian Jasper, whose memorial service I had been to three weeks earlier; Paul Green, Ann's son; Gareth Hughes, who had driven the one-ton vehicle that time when we ate my Mam out of house and home; Colin Parsons, who had shared my trench under the ridge not half a mile away; my best friend, Andrew Walker – 'Yorkie'. My name would have been almost next to his, third from the end.

And there was an unexpected name, 'Scouse' Farrell. He had been in the Medical Corps, but had been seconded to us. He'd joined my platoon just before we landed. He was the first to get trench-foot. He was a lovely guy, full of humour, and God, did he need it – we gave him hell. He was there to look after us, and he couldn't look after himself! Tore him apart, we did. Really made him feel at home. He took it well. Once he'd been on the receiving end of a few well-directed insults, he knew he was one of us.

I looked around again, feeling the wind bite at my face. For a minute, locked inside my own emotions, I had forgotten that this was more than a memorial to the Task Force and to those who had been buried at sea. It was a cemetery for fifteen men whose families had wished their husbands, brothers and sons to be buried here rather than be taken home.

As I wandered around, with Gary and John, the graves, the flowers, and the words on the simple crosses brought another rush of emotion. Here, with a small flowering bush growing on it, was the grave of one of the best-known victims, Lieutenant-Colonel Jones – always known simply as 'H' – killed while leading the attack on the hill above Darwin. One headstone read: 'Colin, we believe life and death are one, even as the river and sea are one.' Another recalled a family saying: 'Darling, you must have been a very good penny.'

One simple memorial said, 'To our dearest husband and father', from a wife and two children. That did for me. I stood there, hiding the tears, thinking, 'I could have been here, alone.' I imagined James fatherless; Lucy alone. What could be worse than being alone – me here, them there? It was too close to bear, almost as if I should have been here, buried or remembered on the plaque.

Gary and John are hard men, but they too felt the power, the *rightness*, of the place. There were no Scots Guards buried there, but there were four from John's unit, 2 Para – three killed at Goose Green, and 'That's for Fred Slough,' said John, pointing. Francis Slough – 'but we always called him Fred' – had been in John's platoon. He was shot on Wireless Ridge, within hours of the end of the war.

Once, it would have seemed odd to me that families should have chosen to have their loved ones buried abroad. I would like to think that if I'd been killed on land, my family would have brought me back to Nelson. But having seen this place, I could understand. There are memorials to British soldiers all over the world, all well looked after by the War Graves Commission. But there is something special about San Carlos. It is a perfect site, and a perfect memorial, beautifully kept by the man who has the best reason of all to undertake the task – Pat Short, the first Falklander to be liberated.

Even in the rain, with the wind gusting cold down from the Sussex Mountains, this place would be beautiful. On a day like this, it was pure magic.

Quite simply, the memorial deserves to be there.

8

GOOSE GREEN

28 November 1991

Returning over the Sussex Mountains the next day, it was John's turn to re-experience the past. Through him, a few hours of vivid, on-the-spot anecdotes, and his dead calm professionalism, I became at last a part of the war.

John, along with the rest of 12 Platoon, part of 2 Para's 'D' Company, was among the first to see action on land. The landings had gone well, despite fierce assaults by the Argentinian Air Force. A dozen Argentinian planes had been shot down for the loss of two ships (*Ardent* and *Antelope*), with four more out of action or damaged. Not bad, considering 10,000 tons of supplies and 3,000 troops were ashore, most of them well dispersed over the cold, wet and windy slopes of the Sussex Mountains to avoid air raids. Now there was nothing to do except wait for transport overland.

John's twenty-six lads, as wet and cold as the peat they dug in, were beginning to suffer with sore feet when the order for action came. They were to clear an area round one of the lonely outposts, Cantera House, on the coast six miles south. This was part of a policy of 'aggressive patrolling' in defence of San

Carlos, but it would also put them within striking distance of Goose Green if necessary. Goose Green, the largest community outside Stanley, was the Argentinian base closest to San Carlos. From there, if anywhere, retaliation would come.

Forward observers had reported seeing three armoured vehicles at Cantera House. They could carry up to thirty-two men each, so there could be quite a force there – more than a match, perhaps, for twenty-six keyed-up young men in their first action.

'Right, lads.' John was a tough task-master, but it was all for their own good. 'Take a brew kit, and only one day's supply of food.'

They were issued three days' rations, but John thought it best for them to lighten their loads. Besides, they would hardly eat in action, and if there were no fighting they'd be resupplied soon enough. Out went everything except dehydrated rolled oats, chocolate drink and apple flakes. Mixing that lot together made a slurry that would keep them going for at least two days. No bergens, no waterproofs because of the noise the material made, and no sleeping-bags. If it rained, they would walk wet, and sleep wet. They'd carry 300 rounds each for the GPMG (general-purpose machine-gun), 100 rifle-rounds each in a bandolier, and another 200 in magazines, grenades, some M66 anti-tank rockets, and spare radio batteries – in all, about sixty to sixty-five pounds per person.

They set off towards dusk on 24 May. It was good to be on the move at last, escaping the drudgery of defence routine. The CO, Lieutenant-Colonel 'H' Jones, came by to send them off. This worried some of the lads – if the CO comes by, well, it's going to be pretty sticky, right, Sergeant?

'Shut up, Minnock, and keep packing.'

There was nothing sinister about 'H's presence. He was a demanding, but fair-minded commander who would want to make sure his men went off properly equipped, properly led and properly motivated.

As night fell, they were taken by helicopter a few miles south, and dropped by a pilot so nervous he went thudding off into the darkness without leaving them their grid reference.

A brief conflab followed with the platoon commander, Jim Barry, to find out where they were. John had known Jim just three months. He was only there by chance. He was a yachtsman, and had been about to go off to compete in the America's Cup, when the Paras' departure from home altered his plans. It had been a close thing – the platoon already had a replacement commander, Jonathan Page, who was put in charge of fire support when Jim Barry returned.

Their position seemed OK. Some small lakes nearby told them they were near enough where they were meant to be – about three miles from Cantera House.

Jim Barry set his compass. They set off. Rain came, driven into their faces by the wind, limiting vision to a metre or two. They were shadows staggering and sliding over the rough ground with their burdens. It was impossible to tell how far they had travelled, until they hit a fence line that should – according to the map – lead them near the house.

The rain eased. There was the dull grey shape of a house. But was it the *right* house? One way to check was for the forward observation officer to use the radio to ask the artillery to fire one round at the house, which was pre-recorded on the artillery's computer-controlled sights. It would be safe enough – one artillery round wouldn't tell the enemy of the Paras' presence.

'Shot out!' came over the radio. 'Forty seconds!' John and Jim Barry fixed their binoculars on the shadow of the house. The seconds ticked by. Then, a good kilometre over to the right, a boom and a flash.

'If that's where Cantera House is, then we're half a k. out to sea,' muttered Jim Barry.

The artillery was way off beam. This was a great boost to confidence. Anyway, the shape ahead had to be Cantera House.

They began a silent approach, planning not to open fire unless fired on. Assuming they weren't seen, they could get in really close, and the shock of the close-quarter assault would win the fire-fight. Divided into sections, each section moved forward, 'went firm', allowed the others to come through, moved forward . . .

The house was empty. Not a trace of the enemy anywhere.

That night, there was no fire, no hot food, no brew, no dry clothing to sleep in, but at least they had cover. Next morning, new orders: they were told to meet the rest of the company and go on to clear Camilla Creek, four miles on towards Goose Green.

They had hardly got to the rendezvous, when the operation was cancelled. More new orders: return to Cantera House. This meant reclearing it, because enemy soldiers might have moved in – another silent approach. Empty, of course. Another night without decent food, dry clothing, or dry boots.

Next morning, three of the lads were casualties – two with bad feet, one with a sprained knee. Jim Barry requested a helicopter. No joy: the weather was 'too bad'. This was rubbish. The day was clear and everyone could see helicopters over the mountains. No use arguing. John and Jim Barry marched the platoon back up the hills, arriving at the top at dusk. The three injured men, all limping in pain, were out of the war. A fourth developed appendicitis that night. Four down, in a minor strategic cock-up almost certainly due to vacillating plans about whether to raid Goose Green or not, while waiting for air transport to get the troops into the Stanley area.

By now, though, plans were hardening. The day before, the *Atlantic Conveyor* had been sunk, together with huge supplies of stores and eight of the helicopters that were going to be used to airlift troops across country. After this, the decision was made that some Commandos and Paras would march overland, while others would be airlifted or shipped as transport became available.

This meant new orders for 2 Para: back down the mountains again, on foot, across eight miles of moorland, to Camilla Creek, then on another four miles to capture Darwin and Goose Green.

It was a risky operation to attempt. The land bridge was only a mile wide, so there would be no outflanking manoeuvres. There was hardly any cover. Planes based at the local airfield at Goose Green would give the Argentinians air cover. There were also Goose Green's 100 civilians to consider. And no one had a clear idea of how many Argentinian troops there were. (In fact, 2 Para was vastly outnumbered, as they discovered later.)

One day's march took the Paras to Camilla Creek, where they stopped for the night, and the following day. That evening John and his platoon, in reserve with the rest of 'D' Company, tabbed over to the operations 'start line' just north of a house called Burntside. The farm itself was being held by about thirty Argentinians who were living in a sheepshed, leaving four civilians in the house. John heard 'A' Company attack – quick rattles of fire, then silence. The Argentinians fled. No one was hurt. Everyone moved on south through the darkness, with two companies taking a shoreline each, and John's company still in reserve.

It started to rain again. 'A' and 'B' Companies assaulted positions on the right and left. Almost at once, John's lot were brought into action too. The Argentinians saw them in the light of the gunfire, and the first bursts came at them, whipping overhead, and slapping into the grass and peat around them.

It was not close-quarter action yet, but it was the first time under fire for most of them. It took Jim Barry as platoon commander and John himself as platoon sergeant to shout and kick the young lads into remembering their drills: 'See the flashes ... Trench to the left, another to the right ... Return fire!'

The drills clicked in. Crack-and-thump: this gave the direction of a shot, the crack of the faster-than-sound round passing overhead, followed by the thump of the gun firing. While one section kept firing, forcing the enemy to keep down, a second section advanced until they were close enough for two men to go in with grenades. At the yell 'Grenade!' everyone hit the deck, boom, a burst of fire, a shout of 'Trench clear!' and on to the next, in a rain-sodden confusion of shouts and fire-bursts and exploding artillery rounds, trench by trench, each one demanding an approach to within a couple of yards, with bullets from your own men zipping in on either side, and flares flaming overhead.

Beyond this first position, at the top of a rise, the immediate limit of exploitation, John, carrying an M79 grenade-launcher, reorganized the men as they came through, checked ammunition, counted heads . . .

There was a section missing.

John went back the way he'd come to look for them, passing through company HQ, failed to find them, and was on his way back when, by the light of mortar flashes, he saw four helmets in silhouette moving along a fence.

Back in company HQ, he asked his company second-in-command, Captain Adams, 'Have we got anyone on our right?'

'I don't think so.'

'Well, there's somebody there.'

Adams ordered up a mini-flare. Four Argentinians stood up. Could be they were trying to surrender, but no one was about to ask questions. John fired his M79.

John took one of his lads over to check the damage. Two had been killed outright, one was injured, and one had got away. The bodies and the wounded man were searched for maps and ammunition – they used 7.62mm ammo, same as the British, so it was standard practice to take it.

The private turned one of the dead men over. He had lost half his face.

'I think he's still alive, Sergeant.'

'Don't be daft. If you think he's still alive, give him the kiss of life.'

John counted twelve trenches 'taken out', before they were held up by the main Argentinian defence line, which straddled the isthmus between Darwin and the ruins of a building known as Boca House. 'A' Company were to take Darwin, 'B' Company the Boca House end and 'D' Company to remain in reserve. The whole operation was meant to be over during the night.

But it wasn't that simple.

Darwin now is a nice little place – half a dozen houses on a level stretch of grass in the lee of hills. The coast bends round into a bay, and on a rise approaching the settlement is a solid dry-stone corral built last century to hold cattle during round-ups. A quarter of a mile to the south is a sharp little hill with a monument on the top.

It was here that 'A' Company's advance stalled, and here that Lieutenant-Colonel 'H' was shot leading a renewed attack on the Darwin end of the defence line. John knew nothing of what had happened, except that the CO was 'down.'

By now 'B' Company, advancing down a bare slope on the Boca House position, had also been stalled.

Boca House then was no more than a few stones. Now, there's nothing at all, except a rolling expanse of well-nibbled grass, smooth as a golf-course, backed by a long gorse bush. Tony, our driver, said the gorse marked the line of an old wall built by gauchos in the last century to keep cattle from escaping during round-ups on Lafonia. The Argentinian position – a trench surrounded by peat walls – was a hundred yards behind the gorse.

Soon after, as daylight came, John's lot started to move round along the shoreline to outflank Boca House. A narrow path allowed John's platoon to advance round the edge of the line, and up through a mine-field. The mines were tagged with orange wire, which would have been invisible at night. Now, in daylight, they were clear enough, and it was safe enough for them to pick their way through. Suddenly there was a blast that flattened everyone. John looked round, his head ringing. One of the boys was sitting up, with some orange wire round his boot and a crater to his side. He was shocked, but not hurt.

'It wasn't me, Sergeant,' he said mournfully.

'It *was* you.' Already some of the others were going across to help him. 'And where do you think you lot are going?'

'To help him, Sergeant.'

'Leave him,' said John flatly, walking gingerly forward. 'He tripped it. He can sort himself out.'

By then, the Argentinians had begun to surrender – about twenty of them, leaving a dozen dead.

The focus of battle moved on, to a building on the outskirts of Goose Green – the school-house; and to the airfield – a flat expanse of grass that spanned a gentle rise ahead. Someone noticed a white flag flying from a peat-wall position on the edge of the airfield. After checking with his commanding officer, Jim Barry said he would take the surrender. Perhaps John should have questioned him (he blamed himself later for not doing so): if the enemy wanted to surrender, they should have been told to come forward. It wasn't up to the Paras to approach. On the other hand, a surrender would save a lot of lives. John simply told two others – Knight and Godfrey – to accompany Jim Barry, with four others to the rear in support.

From a hundred yards away, he saw the men vanish into dead ground and reappear on the rise beyond. Jim approached the position. He seemed to be talking to the Argentinians. Then two other Argentinians approached. Jim was just turning round when from somewhere came a rattle of fire, then another burst, this time from the other side of Jim. He, Knight and Godfrey went down, seeking cover probably – couldn't be too sure from this distance.

Bursts of heavy, accurate small-arms fire made those watching duck down.

'Return fire!'

'But they're shooting at me,' one of the younger lads said plaintively.

'I'm a lot closer than you are, Spencer. If I shoot at you, I'm going to hit you, so bloody well *return fire*!'

John levelled his rifle and fired. No use at this range. The next moment one of the others, Roach, came crawling back over the rise from dead ground. 'I think I've been hit,' he said.

'You *know* if you've been hit.'

'Well, I *think* I've been hit.'

A quick check revealed that a round had split the back of his windproof trousers, and nicked him – the only thing wrong with him was a draft in the basement.

Then Chevill came crawling back. He really had been hit, seriously – once through the shoulder and once in the hip. John delegated Wilson and Roach to give first aid, took a GPMG from one of the gunners and opened up. Several Argentinians fell. He returned the machine-gun to the gunner, told him to give him covering fire, and ran, doubled over, to Knight and Godfrey. As he did so, Barton lobbed a grenade from the M79, and the survivors at the Argentinian position ran off.

Knight and Godfrey were OK.

John crawled up to Jim. He'd taken a burst in the chest. He was dead. John had seen death before, many times, and felt nothing of the shock felt by the inexperienced. Personal feelings had no part in what was going on. But something changes when you lose a commander and a friend. In this case, there was an icy, controlled anger, not just at the loss, but at the circumstances of the loss. Jim Barry had died trying to take a surrender. John hadn't been much of a one to sympathize with the Argentinians before; he would be even warier of such feelings now.

Behind him, the school-house was burning well. Ahead, it was a clear run into Goose Green. From there, he had a good view of the twenty or thirty tin-roofed houses and barns that were scattered along a stubby peninsula and around the shore.

There were no more defensive positions. The battle was as good as over.

They could have gone on, but for some reason were ordered to fall back along the airfield, and dig in, as a protection against the few rounds still coming their way from the village.

It was here that Burridge and Minnock had lucky escapes. John had just told them to reposition themselves. They had begun to stand up, with Burridge moving minutely faster than Minnock, when a bullet whipped above Minnock's back, and then actually sliced straight through Burridge's shoulder harness holding his ammunition, medical kit and poncho. It left a ten-inch graze across his shoulders. A tenth of a second later, the bullet would have cut his spine. As it was, he just went down a lot quicker than he stood up, with a yelp. He took a replacement harness from one of the casualties.

John checked numbers: Jim Barry, Paul Sullivan, and Nigel Smith dead; Chevill wounded.

And Fred Slough and Sheepwash were missing, complete with GPMG and ammunition. No one had any idea where they were. Odd. They could hardly have got shot or blown up in full daylight without anyone noticing.

There was nothing to be done about them, partly because of bullets still flying around, and partly because of action overhead. Three Harriers roared over to bomb positions ahead. An Argentinian plane flew past and fired a burst that cut harmlesly through the position, scaring the life out of the wounded Chevill. Chevill was groggy with morphine and had a saline drip attached to his backside, but he took off across the grass with his trousers round his ankles. They had to catch him to bring him back.

Later, a Pucará came over and dropped napalm, but missed by a long way. Everyone opened up, hit the plane and forced the pilot to bale out, right into the arms of the Paras. (In fact, Carlos had told us in Buenos Aires that the pilot, Cruzado, had been his instructor.)

The next morning, Fred Slough and Sheepwash turned up. An officer had needed a couple of gunners and ordered them to follow him to take out some artillery pieces. Of course, they'd obeyed without question. If John could have got his hands on the officer concerned, he would have done him serious injury. Worse still, they hadn't got anywhere near the artillery, and the officer had left the two squaddies to their own devices. Knowing that if they were to try to return, they might not be recognized, and be shot, they had spent the night under a gorse bush.

That morning came the surrender – a huge crowd of Argentinians gathered on the airfield, 1,200 of them, an astonishing number, three times the whole Para battalion that had assaulted them. They were shepherded into a barn, its black roof overpainted with huge white letters: 'POW'. Barn, roof and letters were still there, untouched, ten years later.

For his young platoon, based in another barn not far from the POWs, just by the airfield, it had been quite a baptism. They'd started out with twenty-six men. Now they were down to twenty. But the action brought benefits. They were battle-hardened, and had mostly proved good lads. John had seen a couple of weak links – the clowns who needed kicking to get them moving. One lad had been badly affected by the action and the deaths, and needed to be kept working for three days solid to prevent him from falling into depression. No one moaned any more about humping ammunition instead of food. All were bitter at how Jim Barry had died, which meant they would not be inclined to be soft on the enemy next time around.

So it wasn't surprising that, once they had dug in to defend Goose Green, they should develop the easy callousness and black humour of all squaddies everywhere.

'Now I understand the theory of crack-and-thump, Sergeant: the crack is when the round hits you – and the thump is when you hit the ground.'

When sixteen Argentinian bodies were lined up on the

ground, boots were seized and tried on – for feet permanently swollen now by wet and cold – and macabre jokes made.

'Hey, look, the Isle of Man sign – three legs, all which way!'

'This guy's face!' – a bullet had passed straight through, causing it to collapse in upon itself – 'The Argentinian girnie champion! Bung a fag in his mouth, and let's have a picture!'

For a few days, they could rest. There was whisky and rum from the locals in exchange for souvenirs from the stockpile of Argentinian weapons, and food brought in by the helicopters, and fags, and sweets.

John, though, needed to stay alert. It was a team he was running, and he had to watch out that everyone was treated fairly. Take the question of sweets. Cigarettes arrived for the smokers, with a random variety of sweets for the seven non-smokers – Mars bars, Twixes and Yorkie bars. He had to remember who had had what, or it was: 'Sarge, why can't I have a Yorkie bar? I had a Mars yesterday.' One day, John meticulously sliced a single Yorkie seven ways to share out with the Marses. Next minute there was a shout: 'Who's eaten my chunk of Yorkie bar?' Uproar. Near mutiny. It sounds petty from lads who had just been through a battle, but they'd not had much for too long, and every little bit counted.

This apart, they were very different young men from those that had set out from Sussex Mountains a few days before.

They would need this hardness on Wireless Ridge, two weeks later.

9

FITZROY

29 November 1991

The return to Fitzroy had been my main aim ever since I knew I was going back to the Falklands. I was sure it would be the most moving part of the trip. I was afraid of the emotions that would hit me when I looked out over the bay where the bomb had struck, and when I saw the memorial to my mates in the Welsh Guards.

I wanted it to be a very private moment, between me and my past – between me and the lads who had never come back. I was pretty sure I wouldn't be able to prevent the tears coming, and equally sure I didn't want this on camera. I had been exposed too much; I didn't fancy the idea of breaking down with the camera focused tight on my face. So, even before we set off from home, I told Malcolm: 'If you want this on film, you've only got one chance. No close-ups, no repeats.' I didn't want anything cheapening the moment for me. As always if I expressed myself forcefully enough, he accepted.

That morning we made the now familiar journey towards Mount Pleasant Airport, doubling back towards the coast a few miles outside Stanley.

For a couple of miles, it was a rough old track, following

the ruts of other Land Rovers, through farm gates, until we rolled into Fitzroy – a dozen scattered houses, a few sheepsheds. One of these, I supposed, was the one I'd been put in briefly after the bomb had struck, but I had no memories to help me identify which. Then on, feeling our way over boggy ground, past the inlet to the south of Fitzroy, up over the grass and bumpy pin-cushion plants on to a rise.

There below was the harbour, Port Pleasant, with a little bay, overlooked by several monuments. Behind us lay Port Fitzroy, the inlet that leads to Bluff Cove, bridged at its narrowest point as a short cut between the two settlements. I had seen virtually nothing of what had gone on ashore, but since then, having seen it, having listened to Gary and John, the past has become part of the present.

John and the other Paras knew there were no Argentinians around when they arrived. They knew because of a now-famous phone call made from Swan Inlet – half-way between Goose Green and Fitzroy – by a small group of Paras who had helicoptered along the coast, flying below thick mist. They were told that the Argentinians had destroyed the Fitzroy-Bluff Cove bridge, and pulled out. They were back at Goose Green with the good news an hour after their departure.

Using the only surviving Chinook to back up their own Scout and SeaKing helicopters, 2 Para were ferried by air from Goose Green, saving another miserable, foot-sore march overland. It was a speedy and dramatic operation – the Chinook took eighty men – that was over in hours. 2 Para were now just thirty miles from Stanley, but exposed, out on a limb, and in need of reinforcements. All the stores and heavy equipment needed would come by sea.

John's platoon dug in. After a dry night, they were ordered to the shore. Then, naturally, Sod's Law came into force – it chucked it down. By the time they arrived at the shore they were soaked. A landing-craft ferried them across the inlet to Fitzroy, where they sheltered in sheepsheds.

They were comfortable enough, warm, and well fed. They'd left most of their kit and bergens behind, but all this gear would be through soon, along with a whole mass of extras inherited from the casualties. A pal of John's from a posting in Kenya the previous year, Taff Reese, had asked him for a roll mat. John had promised one as soon as the casualties' stuff came through.

On 8 June, around midday, Taff had just arrived to pick up his mat, and John had just given it to him, when the jets came over. Nothing particularly odd about this – there had been a good deal of friendly flights over, and there had been no warning of an Argentinian raid.

Meanwhile, more troops were arriving by sea. It was a grim journey. Gary was among the Scots Guards taken half-way by *Intrepid* – not all the way, because this would have left the vessel exposed at dawn. Instead, he and the other Scots Guards were transferred into an open landing-craft twenty miles out to sea, and endured a nightmarish journey – seven hours of spray, rain and wind – round the coast.

Landing in darkness, they tabbed through another downpour to sheepsheds in Bluff Cove. Here, the next day, conditions improved. The sheepsheds offered a dry base. From here, the Guards were circulated out to two entrenched positions: one on a nearby rise overlooking the bay, and the other off in the opposite direction, on low ground. Even outside, they kept warm, because they were expecting air attack, and spent a couple of days building peat walls ten inches thick, which was what it would take to resist thirty-millimetre cannon fire.

They all told each other it was only a matter of time before an attack. The Argentinians were that close, up on Mount Harriet, eight miles away.

Next in line round the coast from San Carlos were the Welsh Guards in *Fearless*, yours truly included. Some 250

Welsh Guards made the same horrible journey in landing-craft. Luckily (or unluckily as it turned out) for me, I didn't have to endure this. There weren't enough landing-craft for us all, so we returned to San Carlos in *Fearless*. The next day, we boarded the *Sir Galahad*, already being loaded with Rapier rocket-launchers, vehicles and men from Field Ambulance and 5 Brigade's medical unit.

The two Welsh Guards commanders were told the destination was Bluff Cove, off Port Fitzroy. The ship was then to return to Port Pleasant to unload the Rapiers and Field Ambulance.

This was where *Galahad*'s troubles started.

We were soon aboard, but it took another six hours to finish loading. This time I spent happily settled on the open deck, which was like a car deck on a Channel ferry. By now it was well into the night. There was a risk we might not make it by dawn, so the orders changed: now we were to head for Port Pleasant, which would save travelling the last few miles.

But then what? Were the Welsh Guards also to land at Port Pleasant, ten miles from our final destination? No one said, and no one realized the hole in the plans.

We reached Port Pleasant after the 150-mile journey round the coast at about 8 a.m. It had been a clear, moonlit night, and it was a clear, bright day. There was no sign of any Argentinian aircraft – perhaps their spirit had been broken.

The day before there had been six landing-craft at Port Pleasant. By now, though, there was only one, plus a small pontoon raft.

The majors in command of landing operations at once saw the danger of leaving us all aboard. They had a solution: we could pile on to the raft and get towed ashore. Then we could tab across country to Bluff Cove.

This would have meant a tiring march and separation from our heavy equipment. Besides, we had been told we were getting a ride all the way to Bluff Cove. Our commander, Major 'Gunner' Sayle – always known by his nickname because his initials were G.N.R. – didn't want us messed about like this and exposed to danger out in the open without our defences.

Only at noon was a decision made: we would all be ferried round the corner in the landing-craft. But again we were delayed, because the Field Ambulance claimed priority. Another hour was lost getting them ashore. This at least gave the blokes ashore some defences – the Rapier rocket-launchers.

Then, to cap it all, came another problem. The loading ramp of the landing-craft became stuck. We would all have to climb down into the craft, after our gear was loaded by crane. Another delay.

We had been sitting there, in the clear light of day, and in full view of Argentinian troops up on Mount Harriet, for five hours – time enough for a message to get to Stanley, to Buenos Aires, and to Carlos's group in Río Gallegos.

Like a true squaddie, I was keen to get back down below to have a cup of tea. Tea and sticky buns – what could be better than that, instead of being outside getting our arses wet? We knew we had been on board a long while, but it really didn't register that we were in danger.

If only I could have had a quick word with Gary, dug in on his rise three miles away to the north. He knew well enough, because the day before two Skyhawks had had the cheek to try to shoot him up – him and a few others. The first time over, they were past before the Guards could grab weapons, but they were foolish enough to come around for a second go. Everyone and everything opened up: machine-guns, rifles, pistols, the lot. The first plane ran slap into a wall of metal, wobbled, smoked and crashed into the sea. The second plane veered off double quick.

The next day, 8 June, was even better for air attacks. It was the first really pleasant day Gary had seen. Compared with the misery of previous days, this was like midsummer. The guys took turns to dry out shirts and boots in the sun, ready for action at any moment, because in weather like this it would be crazy for the Argentinians not to attack. It was 'any minute now' right through the morning. Gary knew there was a resupply ship of some sort over the hill in Port Pleasant, but it never occurred to anyone that there would be troops on board.

So it was no great surprise when Carlos popped over the hills from the west and zoomed the length of Port Fitzroy. Of course, he was after ships, not troops, so he and his squadron were out over the water, and not at too much risk from the Guards' small-arms.

Seconds later, Carlos was banking to the right out over the sea when he spotted us, and turned into his bombing run.

When they heard the *boom!* the Paras in John's shed ran to defensive positions outside. Carlos was gone, but John and the others were in time to open up on the last three, forcing them to bank away. Scots Guards and Paras alike saw the smoke of the *Galahad* rising over the bay, but no one except those on the spot knew until much later that troops had been still on board. When they learned, it came as a huge shock. As Gary said, everyone knew – the soldiers knew, the civilians knew, even the *sheep* knew – that the Argentinian planes would be coming.

I changed into white shirt, Guards tie, blazer with Guards buttons, and grey trousers. I was determined to do this properly, and waited slightly apart as the crew set up the camera.

There were five memorials in all – three on the slope to my right, one straight ahead, and another the other side of the little bay. The number surprised me. I had been expecting just one – the one directly below me, which I could see was in honour of the Welsh Guards, because it was topped by a Celtic cross, with arms of equal length set in a circle.

Malcolm caught my eye, and nodded. As I started my march down towards the Welsh Guards' memorial, I found my mind still on the camera behind me. A silly thought struck me: what if I tripped, rolled down the slope, made myself look a complete idiot on camera? I squared my shoulders, and kept a measured pace.

Approaching the memorial I forgot the camera. Sadness touched me – a foretaste of what I expected when I saw the list of names. The wind was gusting from the south, over the low ridge the other side of the bay, but there were enough breaks in the cloud for occasional filtered sunlight to take the chill off and touch the dull brown landscape with gold. To my left lay the open Atlantic, and to my right lowlands rolling over towards Mount Pleasant. A bird high above me uttered shrill peeping cries.

Strangely, at this point, it was not sadness that filled my mind. I found myself staring round curiously, my mind filling with questions. Where exactly in the bay had the *Galahad* been lying? Where was I brought ashore? Where were we supposed to land? I couldn't remember. It had all happened so quickly. Perhaps I'd never known. Now I never would know. It struck me as odd to have come all this way, to be so close to the past, and yet not to be able to answer a few simple questions.

The memorial stood on a rocky headland some twenty feet above the little cove, which dropped away to the right. The stone was Welsh, too, I remembered. It came from Gelligaer Quarry, a mile or so up the road from Nelson. Twelve wreaths lay at the base, left over from Remembrance Sunday almost a month before.

Below the cross was a braided pattern, and below that again ran the names.

I started to read the names:

Burke, Carlyle, Dale, Dunphy, Edwards

– the old familiar names –

Elley, Gibby, Grace, Green, Griffiths.

How old was the oldest then – on 8 June 1982? Twenty-four, perhaps? 'They grow not old –

Hughes, Hughes, Jasper, Keeble

– as we that are left grow old' –

Kedghane, Marks, Mordecai, Newbury, Nicholson
– but they would have liked the chance to grow old. I
was lucky –
Parsons, Phillips, Poole, Rowberry, Sweet
– I would see my son grow up –
Thomas, Thomas, Thomas, Thomas
– I would grow old –
Walker (Sleep on, Yorkie)
– be remembered by my children, by my children's children –
Ward, Weaver, Wigley, Williams.
And no 'Weston', because I was lucky – I would be in
a country churchyard back home, not here listed in stone
between Weaver and Wigley, not two miles out to sea and
half a mile down.

'*Yn angof ni chant fod*' read the inscription underneath –
'We will remember them'.

I was alone with the memorial, the water and the moorlands.
I felt the wind through my blazer, and looked up. It was much
the same now as it was then: blue sky, scattered cloud, bit of
a wind.

I turned away, and walked along the path that skirted the
little bay. A lone cormorant watched from the rocks, and the
waves gently lapped the white sand. I looked briefly at the other
memorials: one to men of the Royal Fleet Auxiliary, and three
private crosses – including one to Gareth Hughes, the driver
of my section.

One final look out to sea. It was strange – the rush of
emotion I had been expecting had not come. There were
no ghosts, no sudden memories. I still couldn't work out
where we had been lying. I didn't see the two ships lying
out there, the landing-craft shuttling back and forth. No
screams, smoke, explosions. Anyone standing at this point
on 8 June would have seen Carlos's Skyhawk streaking in
from the left. It would have been easy enough to imagine it

– but I didn't. Meeting Carlos, experiencing the shock of the San Carlos memorial, remembering the landing – all this had already almost completely eroded the burden of the past.

No, my past was not here after all. My purpose in coming had been mostly fulfilled before I ever arrived.

10

THE ARGENTINIAN CEMETERY

29 November 1991

A task remained to be done, a promise to be fulfilled: back in
Buenos Aires, Ignacio had asked me to honour the graves of his
countrymen buried on the Falklands. The flowers themselves
had been seized by customs in Chile, but there was nothing to
prevent me fulfilling the spirit of the request, except one thing:
Malcolm wanted to film me doing it.

Once again, I found myself caught in a conflict between
what I wanted and the demands of filming. I didn't mind at
all about placing flowers on Argentinian graves, if I was doing
a favour to Ignacio. Standing in for those who couldn't make
the journey themselves – that was fine, as a private individual.
But it wouldn't *look* all that reverent, because that wasn't how
I felt. I didn't want to give the impression that this was me,
personally, honouring the graves of those who had killed our
lads. If I did, I was sure there were many people back home
who would find it offensive.

Malcolm said that it was my decision, and I was in a
quandary.

It had turned into a beautiful day as we retraced the now
familiar track towards Goose Green and Darwin, but still I felt

the pressure building. Once again, I was two people: a very private person committed to my own personal journey; but also a very public person making a film, and very committed to the person making that film. I didn't know how I was going to handle it.

For the first time, the sun shone hot from a clear blue sky. Tony turned off the track and led us off over the grass for a few hundred yards, rolling down into a shallow valley, sheltered from the breeze. We lay out on the long, clumpy grass. A line of hills blocked the view ahead. A jet from MPA cut across the sky, low down, following the crest of the hills. As its roar died away, silence returned. Apart from an abandoned house a few hundred yards away, there was neither sign nor sound of another human being.

We were back on the track again, swerving around road-building equipment and piles of newly scraped earth. The government was spending a fortune on this road, and it wasn't even going to stretch all the way over the Sussex Mountains to San Carlos. Apparently, it was ending on the west coast, a few miles north of Darwin. There was going to be a new ferry terminal for the link to West Falkland. But at the moment there were only a few dozen people in this part of East Falkland, and not many more across the sound in West Falkland. Who would be using the road? Tourists? Oil-workers?

In any event, the road was part of coming change. Change wouldn't be all bad. Not long ago, kids in the 'camp' were raised only to work. I heard of one man, only fifty years of age, who had started work for the Falkland Islands Company at the age of nine. For five pounds a month, he lived on an outlying island with a couple of teenagers for months at a time. He had virtually no education. There was a travelling teacher, but he never went out to the island.

Yet he and his wife still loved the isolation they were used to, and the road would mean an end to all that, at least around here. Today's kids are drawn to Stanley, because that's where the work is. San Carlos has shrunk. The patterns of sheep-farming are changing. Perhaps when the road is built San Carlos will die completely.

I wouldn't like to live like this, but there was something special about this isolation. I could imagine hordes of tourists tearing about the hills in cross-country vehicles. This is one of the world's last truly wild places, and there's enough of the romantic in me to feel a little sad at the passing of a way of life – and the passing, perhaps, of a wilderness.

To our right now, a high peak was coming into view, a flat-topped ridge of rock. The last time we made the trip it had been covered in cloud.

'Mount Usborne,' said Tony. It was 2,300 feet high – the highest on the islands. He said there was a big black lake behind it that was very beautiful and hardly ever seen by anyone. He planned to explore it some day.

We dropped down towards an inlet of the sea. Up to our left, on top of a bluff, lay the Argentinian War Memorial. Its position was well chosen, because it looked over the inlet to Goose Green and Darwin, the scene of the Paras' success in the first land action of the war. To our right as we slowed at the bottom of the rise lay Burntside, the start line for the Battle of Goose Green. There were some workmen converting it into lodgings for road-workers. It wasn't surprising it needed work, when you consider what happened there in the war.

We swung left, up a steep rise, and on to gently sloping grassland. There lay a small field of white crosses, surrounded by a white fence, squared off – a neat splash of white against the carpet of grass.

Though this was one of the few places you could drive without fear of becoming bogged down, the setting was wilder than San Carlos – and just as spectacular. The cemetery tilts inland towards the long flat ridge of Usborne and the Sussex Mountains. Over to the left there was a slight dip. This was where we had meandered over to San Carlos. Usborne was fifteen miles away, but you could see its grey flanks as clearly as if you were looking through a telescope. In between, and to right and left, swept the brown and yellow grassland.

The cemetery itself holds 230 crosses, in neat rows, all heading little gravel graves divided by well-trimmed grass. At the top of the field stands a larger white cross.

It was a peaceful setting, enough to make me feel a proper respect, even though these were Argentinian graves. As the engines died, however, an incongruous sound rose above the breeze. Three burly men were re-laying one of the grass verges. One of them, a bearded character in a rasta hat from St Helena, was singing his head off to the radio. It was playing the Monty Python song from the film *Life of Brian*: 'Always look on the bright side of life'. Gary and John had not been all that keen on the idea of coming here in the first place. Now the awful, cheery song –

> Always look on the bright side of death,
> Even when you take your ultimate breath

– inspired in them a brief and tasteless reversion to squaddie black humour. I understood. They had fought against some of the men buried here, and almost certainly killed several of them personally. ('I think this is one I prepared earlier,' muttered Gary.) They had seen some of their own comrades killed, possibly by bullets fired by one of the dead Argentinians. Everything had been done in the line of duty, and there was no hatred in them, but the idea of honouring enemy graves didn't seem right, especially as Gary was still serving.

Fortunately, I had good reason to disown them, because one of the grave-diggers, a Geordie, recognized me, and asked me to pose with him while his mates took a snap.

The crew was getting ready. The radio was switched off. I walked among the graves. There had been an official visit from family members in Argentina back in March. Despite the wind that battered this exposed spot, most of the crosses still had dried flowers fixed to them and beads draped around them. Odd, because over half the graves had no name. On most crosses, the words in English ran: 'An Argentinian soldier known only to God'. It seemed the visiting families, unable to find a grave with their own son's name on it, had simply adopted one.

John and Gary knew well enough why so many hadn't been identified. It wasn't simply that the bodies had no name-tags; quite often, there hadn't been enough of the body left to make up an individual. And if there were only 230 buried here, what had happened to the bodies of the other 100 identified on the memorial back in Buenos Aires? Were they the ones that people said had been burned over near Stanley? And again the thought came to me: how many others had there been burned, buried in trenches or dumped at sea? This was the only grave for Argentinians on the islands, yet Argentinians had died in many places. There must, at some time, have been many, many more.

Anyway, it was good that the powers that be had done their bit for these kids, whoever they were. Each one had been some mother's son, and he hadn't deserved death on a cold and barren place he had never wished to visit, let alone fight for.

Now Malcolm wanted to film, and my inner conflict gripped me again. I was keen to fulfil my promise to Gorriti, but was very wound up about being filmed doing it. The other two lads didn't have any problem – when Malcolm asked them, they chose not to accompany me. It was down to me, and I simply couldn't find an easy solution.

In the end, I did it both ways – and neither way. I was going to fulfil my promise. I couldn't allow the presence of a camera to prevent me from doing that. And I felt under too much of an obligation to Malcolm to refuse to be filmed.

I picked up the dried flowers, and walked up the centre of the cemetery, collar up to protect the back of my neck from the sun. At the cross, I was a little reassured to see that I was not the first from Britain to honour the Argentinian dead. A poppy wreath, with the crossed swords of the British Army, had been nailed to the cross. I should, perhaps, have laid the flowers gently and stood for a moment in silence. If the camera hadn't been running, if I hadn't felt any pressure, I'm sure I would have done.

As it was, with a quick gesture that expressed the turmoil I felt, I dropped the flowers down at the foot of the cross, then turned and walked away.

11

ATTACK AND DEFENCE

29 November 1991

A funny thing happened back in Stanley that evening. After
the double strain of the visits to Fitzroy and the Argentinian
Cemetery, I could have done without it.

Gary and I had been having a drink or two up at the
Victoria. It had been a good evening, with everyone very
friendly, because by now a lot of people knew me. 'But Simon,'
Gary would say, acting surprised, 'what I can't understand is
– how do they *recognize* you?' Cheeky sod. Anyway it was
getting towards closing time, and they're super-strict about
that down there. I don't know why – perhaps it's one of
the few things they can be strict about. We had promised
to show ourselves at Deano's as well. As Gary was deep in
conversation, I said I'd hurry on down and get our orders in
before closing time.

So there I was at the bar, on my own, ordering, when it
happened.

Now, perhaps I should have been warned. There had been
a lot of conversations, so many I can't remember, and I'd been
free enough with my opinions about the Falklands. Naturally,
I had never said I found it a heaven on earth. No one took

offence. But there had been this one guy who, after talking for a bit, said: 'You're so friendly!'

'Is that a surprise, butt?'

'Well, yes, sort of. I heard someone say you were a bit anti.'

A bit anti? I had probably said at some point that I didn't think the place was me, that I found it a bit bleak, and a bit small, and I didn't think I'd be coming back. I certainly never intended to give offence, because all the people I'd spoken to had been wonderful. In that case, it was nothing, over as soon as raised. But later I realized: there are always people ready to take offence. I was talking to one of them right then.

'You won't have time to drink up,' said the barmaid aggressively, when I ordered.

'Oh, I think we will.'

'Who do you think you are,' she said with sudden anger that had me staring at her open-mouthed, 'coming down here, pretending to know all about us? I saw more action than you did anyway.'

She slammed the drinks down, took my money and backed off, leaving me to take the glasses through to another room, to Gary, who had just arrived.

'I do not believe what that bird just said to me,' I muttered, and passed on her words. As I did so, I really began to see red. What the hell did she mean, she *saw more than me*? She could have been no more than a kid in the war. Gary was trying to play it cool, but I was getting more and more steamed up.

The police were outside now, to ensure closing, and we were soon leaving. To do so, we went back through the bar, and there she was.

'Hey,' I said. I couldn't help it. I had to say something. 'There's no need for that sort of talk. There's . . .'

'You saw nothing!' She was shouting now. 'I was at Goose Green, and I saw more of the war than you saw!'

I really lost my rag then: 'You call being burned like this
"*nothing*"?'

'You didn't even *meet* any Falkland Islanders!' she went on.
'There were other soldiers hurt besides you, you know. Why
should you get all the attention?'

I couldn't believe it. I didn't ask to go down there, I didn't
ask to get burned, didn't ask to have the documentaries made
about me. I find myself a public figure, and people ask me
questions, and I reply as honestly as I can, and be as friendly
as I know how, and then it all backfires, out of the blue, as
if she couldn't bear the fact that I was a real character, with
my own opinions. Now she saw that I was a human being, not
some simpering wimp, some injured dog she could slobber over,
something seemed to explode in her. Here she was blaming me,
full of resentment, not a flicker of sympathy or gratitude – to
me or all the other lads – that she and her family had been
rescued from Argentinian rule. Not that I expected garlands
of love and joy, but I certainly didn't deserve to be virago'd
and castigated by a barmaid who'd been a kid at the time.

There was no arguing with her, no point in arguing. I couldn't
accept this right then, and kept trying to get through to her, but
at least Gary could see sense, and somehow got me to leave.
'Why did she *say* that?' I kept repeating, 'Why did she *say*
that?' I couldn't understand what she was talking about. The
anger I felt was as much surprise and shock at her unfairness.
God, I had seen action! I had suffered! True, I hadn't actually
killed anyone – was that what she blamed me for? True, I'd
tried to save lives – would she have been happier if I hadn't?
Or was it the fact of my survival that bothered her? Would
she rather I were dead?

Back at the hotel, Malcolm and the others began to talk me
down. It took a while – an hour, two hours, I don't know –
but gradually I relaxed. With their help, I saw that my feelings
-- anger at being insulted, self-righteous indignation at being
unfairly accused – were not the point.

'Use it,' Malcolm kept saying of the whole episode. 'Use it.'

Eventually I saw what he meant. I could never have argued her out of her anger even if we'd talked all night. She had something in her mind, and she was sticking to it. I should have seen that. Besides not being a killer, and surviving, my third mistake — joking apart — had been to take her seriously. I should never have got angry, should never have engaged. There would always be people out there wanting to have a go. Anyone with experience of being in the public eye ought to know this.

Especially me, especially now. As Gary said, 'You better get ready for it, because you don't know what will be coming your way after the programme goes out. You ought to be able to take this sort of thing, and let it roll off.'

True, very true. I would have to do better, because it would happen again sooner or later.

1 December 1991

Sooner, as it happened.

Two days later, a Saturday, Gary and I had been to the disco. It must have been about 1 a.m. We were on our way out, along with a cheerful crowd. The mood was good, as usual, because most of the crowd knew us by now, but outside the door — Gary remembered later — there were two girls looking daggers at me. He could see something was up. And this time it wasn't quite out of the blue — we had seen the two of them before, at one of Deano's karaoke nights. They were loud, very loud. We came surging through the door, and suddenly I was aware of this massive yeti creature in front of me. Faith, her name was. I swear she was almost as big as me, with short fair hair and jeans, looking a good deal tougher than her squaddie boyfriend.

'Hey,' she said. 'You saw nothing! You did nothing in the war! What makes you so great?'

She was drunk, and spoiling to have a go. Obviously she

and the barmaid had got together, because their words were so similar. And obviously she was expecting to get the same sort of reaction from me. People crowded round. Gary, who knows what's what in close-quarter combat, wasn't going to give me a chance to repeat my reactions of two nights before.

'Don't you talk about the war,' he said to her. 'You may have been in it, but Simon's wearing it.'

'Only his head and his hands,' she shouted.

'And his back, and his stomach and his chest.'

'Don't give me that shit!' She turned to me: 'What do you want, sympathy? You're rich, you are! You drive a BMW and a Mercedes!'

'Well, actually, he drives a Peugeot 205,' said Gary mildly.

'I don't want to hear that!' she yelled. 'You only look like that because you want to!'

'Oh?' To my relief, I realized I was not in the least angry. It's wonderful what a little training can do. 'You think I wanted to have forty-six operations?' I asked calmly. Not being angry was a relief. I could see her for what she was. I could see the viciousness and anger in her; I could see how simply accepting the attack would make it harmless.

'My sister's a nurse and she told me you can change your face.'

'You're right,' I said. 'You're absolutely right.'

'She knew someone who was burned, and he looks perfect now!'

'You're right,' I said again. Obviously she knew nothing about plastic surgery. I knew now there was no way she could get to me. 'You know all about my life. You know me better than I know myself.'

Poor girl, now she was looking foolish, and she knew it, and this made her really wild. 'You just keep looking like that to *make money*!'

'You know best,' I repeated reasonably. Two nights earlier,

the accusation would have stung me. Tonight, it stung someone else.

Gary saw this girl nearby draw her arm way back and throw a punch like he'd never seen anyone throw before. Her fist must have travelled six feet. Before I knew it, this fist flew past me and landed Faith a crack in the chops. Anyone else would have fallen. I would have, probably. But Faith just rocked back, and then lunged forward.

I looked round. My protector, Cathy, clearly had it in for Faith anyway, and had been driven into a fury by the suggestion that I was cashing in on my face. She was much smaller, but looked pretty ferocious. Gary caught hold of her, and held her back, swinging her round and buckling her knees, and then protecting her with his back from Faith's retaliation.

Now Faith was grabbed by some of the crowd, and started thrashing about, like a caged animal, shouting 'Let me get at her! Let me get at her!' and Cathy was looking as wild as a tiger, but Gary was already handing her over to her boyfriend and telling him to take her away.

Faith suddenly seemed to decide enough was enough, and started to back off. She made a final lunge, to be blocked by Gary. 'Stop it,' he said. 'It's not worth it.'

There was one final explosion when Cathy reappeared holding a bottle, looking as if she really meant business, but Gary sorted this out as well. Then Faith was on her way, almost as if nothing had happened, and Cathy was lost in the crowd with her boyfriend, and everyone started to disperse. People were apologizing for the whole thing, hoping I didn't think this was the way all Falkland Islanders behaved.

No apologies needed. I was beginning to see the funny side. Faith had been so wild she had made a complete fool of herself. As we walked back to the hotel, I began to feel sorry for her. I would be on my way home soon, but she would have to stay on in a small community where everyone knows everything, living with the consequences of what she was and what she had done.

12

TUMBLEDOWN

2 December 1991

Gary and John had begun to fill the last hole in my experience. The stream of jokes and stories had reminded me of life as a squaddie; I'd seen Goose Green; but I still hadn't really understood what they had been through. For this I had to wait until our last day, when the filming was over, and we had time to walk the windy battlegrounds of Tumbledown and Wireless Ridge.

The plan had been to attack Stanley on 8–9 June, but the *Galahad* disaster, among other logistical problems, forced delays. Delay was dangerous. The Argentinian troops were well dug in, well prepared and their base in Stanley was close. They could wait; we couldn't. Our men were at the point of a supply line stretching back to San Carlos, and beyond to ships at sea, to Ascension, to the RAF bases in England. Delay risked injuries from exposure and losses of food, equipment, ammunition and men, all of which would be hard to make good.

The plan called for a two-stage battle: Longdon, Two Sisters and Harriet to be taken on one night. Then, with artillery carried forward in support, 2nd Battalion Scots Guard were to take Tumbledown, with the Gurkhas following through to take Mount William. In the north, 2 Para were to take Wireless Ridge. The whole plan was risky. If it were to fail, exposure would take its toll. There were few reserves. Failure at this point might mean negotiating a settlement with the Argentinians.

Longdon, Two Sisters and Harriet all fell on 11–12 June for the loss of twenty-three men. A good start. A day's delay followed, to allow time to complete reconnaissance, but already the RAF, the Navy and artillery were battering Tumbledown and Wireless Ridge. The Scots Guards were helicoptered up from Bluff Cove to dig in behind a low rise known as Goat Ridge. Gary, second-in-command of his section, which was part of Left Flank Company, which was one of the battalion's three companies, was one of the first arrivals. Just before dropping into the dead ground below Goat Ridge, he was heartened by the sight of Tumbledown, two miles ahead, lit up by explosions. The Argentinians would be lucky to have any survivors at all up there.

As the Wessexes thumped back and forth, artillery and mortar shells rained in. Surrounded by the roar of planes and the boom and crash of artillery, the Guards dug hard, fast and deep. It rained, near-freezing rain. Not that you notice being cold and wet in the middle of an artillery barrage. No one cared about the water in the trenches any more – better wet than dead.

Once the trenches were dug, the Argentinian artillery would not have been a major worry. You could hear the explosion in the gun, and would know that forty seconds later the shell would land. Plenty of time to take cover. Except that every ten minutes a helicopter would land, ironing out the sound of the gun firing. By pure luck, only one man was injured.

Tumbledown was out of sight, but the Guards were well briefed about what lay ahead. The mountain was a long spine of rock, 650 feet high, its upper slopes made of sharp pinnacles jutting up from an extraordinary, steep shield of rock, smooth as a tortoise-shell. At its edges, the shell broke into huge boulders that gave good cover. Below, a succession of tortuous rock rivers divided rough fields of grass and peat. Other troops lay invisible in dozens of trenches and foxholes. The Argentinians were well entrenched – or rather had been, before the bombardment. From the sound of things, there wouldn't be many of them left.

After dark, the battalion moved up to the bottom of the ridge, waiting, with all three companies – Left Flank, Right Flank and 'G' – in position. They fixed bayonets: they'd heard the story of a guy without a bayonet coming up against an Argentinian, squeezing the trigger, only to find his magazine was empty. Click. The Argentinian picked up his weapon and shot him dead. No Scots Guard was going to make that mistake.

From a mile away, the sound of battle – a diversionary attack to the south, towards Mount William. It was then, waiting, as the cold began to seep into him, that Gary's feelings sharpened. Fear was part of it. Like everyone else, in case anything were to happen to him, Gary had written his last letter home, and given it to a mate. Anyone who says they don't feel fear at this point is a liar. But there was more than fear – there was anticipation and excitement. He was just lying there, looking up at the clear sky, having a last fag, when a shooting-star flashed overhead. He'd seen a couple before. There's nothing mystical about Gary, but the stars suddenly seemed like good omens. He felt he would be OK. He was eager to get into action.

After half an hour or so the move came, in silence – radio silence as well. Reports of progress would be carried by runners. The commander of Left Flank, Major John Kiszley, stepped forward, and shadows shifted in the darkness. You only knew the operation had begun when the man next to you moved. The recce platoon eased forward, leaving torches pointing back and down to mark the way. 'G' Company led on, across the official start line – a fence – to take out the first heavy machine-gun post, leaving the three platoons of Left Flank to follow when the position was clear.

Almost at once, the British artillery, mortars and machine-guns opened up from behind and from Mount Harriet on the right, to give any survivors on Tumbledown something to think about while the infantry moved silently forward.

A shadow – a runner reporting back. 'G' Company had reached the machine-gun post. No one there. Great. They'd all been killed, or fled. Perhaps the whole mountain had been abandoned. Left Flank moved forward to 'G' Company, through them, and on.

But only for fifty metres. The enemy hadn't all gone. They were right there. Gary and the rest of his company were almost on them when they were seen.

Suddenly, a new and shocking reality. Games, rehearsals, training, talk, briefings, all the knowledge, nothing prepares you for the reality. From a few yards ahead, a single burst of fire, and then twenty, thirty bursts, a wall of red-hot tracer. The only response – flatten yourself. Find any possible cover: a stone, a mound of earth, anything. Novices instantly learn a new skill – how to collapse your chest one extra inch. White light above. You see the enemy, they see you. A shooting gallery. Bullets inches above your head, rocks cracking into shrapnel beside you, a man shot through his cap-star a few yards away.

Incredible. All that bombardment, yet they had survived – more than survived. Gary showed me why. He led me up into the high slopes, right under the edge of the strange smooth shell of rock. There was a cave, still littered with boots, cartridge cases, wire. It was a natural air-raid shelter. In fact, all along the mountain, the boulders and crags had all made superb shields. Despite the massive twenty-four-hour barrage, the Argentinians had sustained only one casualty. All that sophisticated weaponry, all that money, and at the end of the day, it was down to the man with a bayonet.

For long seconds, a minute, two minutes, nothing but shock, noise, confusion. Then the training began to work. Shock died. Adrenalin flowed. Exhilaration, and fear, and so many emotions, and you couldn't afford any of them, because the only way to survive was: return fire. Crawl forward. Form sections. *Win the fire-fight.*

To help, according to the textbook, the company commander would call in a 'creeping barrage', with artillery landing shells fifty metres ahead. Then the Guards would advance, and take the position trench by trench, foxhole by foxhole.

But no textbook ever prepares you for what actually happens. Artillery rounds ahead, yes. But there were rocks. Metal shrapnel, rock shrapnel. Men being hit by shrapnel, Jesus – their *own* shrapnel. A rogue barrel landing shells in among their own men. All the barrels were controlled by computer. The only way to discover the rogue was to retrain the lot at a safe spot and test-fire them in sequence. That would take time.

No more artillery. The attack lost momentum, perhaps the most crucial element in any attack, and stalled, halted, broke into a collection of half a dozen small battles. Now it was down to section commanders to win their own fire-fights.

The enemy soldiers in the rocks above and ahead were jubilant. These were the men under Carlos Vazquez, who had talked so graphically and emotionally to Gary in Buenos Aires. In the darkness between flares, one over-confident character even shouted out in English: 'Surrender to the Argentinian Army!' He stood up to shout it, making himself visible in night-viewing devices. Idiot. A hail of fire, a scream, and down he went. He must have been dead on arrival at the floor of his trench.

A trench thirty-five metres in front of Gary and his section. But the trench had a wall of rock. Automatic fire couldn't get through. He needed an M66 anti-tank rocket to destroy the trench. But the guy with the launchers was behind, pinned down by enemy fire. No help from the section to the left

– out of shouting range. And the section commander didn't want to move.

Gary said to him: 'Look, we have to take them out.'

'No. Leave it! Leave it!'

He only wanted to survive. But they all wanted to survive, and to survive some action had to be taken. If you don't get them, they'll get you – in this case, by cutting between the two sections. Each second's delay increased the danger.

Impossible to move, must move.

'We *have* to take them out!'

'Then you'll have to do it.'

Everyone looking at him, the section's No. 2. The looks said: what do we do? Suddenly, he was alone. No one to help, no one else to look to. The immediate, urgent desire: to keep down, hide, vanish. Fear of moving, because it risked death right now; but not moving meant death later; *if you don't get them, they'll get you*. Must lead, must lead by example. Can't move, must move ... until one thing broke through – fear of showing fear to others. Only one thing to do: face the fear. Survival, his survival, the survival of them all, depended right at that moment on his bravado. No, not bravery, he was no braver than anyone else. He just knew, with certainty, what had to be done, and there was no one else to do it.

Move!

Crawl near enough to the guy with the M66 for him to toss over a launcher, crawl back, fire the rocket. That got their heads down. Make the rest of the section keep firing. Crawl forward, flash a red warning torch back to the lads to stop covering fire, toss in a phosphorus grenade, reach over with the self-loading rifle, fire off a magazine to stop them picking up the grenade and tossing it back.

Phosphorus grenades are nasty things. The phosphorus, which clings to every splinter of metal, burns anything it touches. Even a fragment landing gently on your hand will burn straight through in seconds. So after one explodes in a trench, there's a hiss and smell of scorched flesh, followed by a final burst of fire, just to make sure.

The log-jam broke. It was fourteen below, and snow was beginning to gust across the slopes, but no one was aware of this, with the adrenalin flowing, the section moving as a team, pepperpotting forward, following this madman doing crazy things.

Gary was not alone in this. All three of the other section commanders were later mentioned in dispatches. He was in a world where every man in authority had to act crazy to make others do the same. All around, a dozen, a score of crazy men, acting as though they were invulnerable, ran, crept, fired, threw, ran, crept, fired . . .

Near him men were dying on both sides. At one point in the light of a flare, Gary saw a man shot, a glimpse of horror, taking a tracer in the stomach. Tracers are made luminous by phosphorus. The man saw the bullet enter. He knew the bullet would simply fry his insides. In instantaneous reaction, he plunged his whole hand into the open wound to seize the bullet. He sank to his knees, and died, kneeling, his hand still lodged inside his stomach, and a look of horror on his face.

On, taking out trench after trench, ducking from rock to rock. The trenches are still there, and so are some of the rocks. One had received a direct hit from a mortar. A soldier had been sheltering behind it. The rock had exploded, blasting the soldier with a rain of rock splinters. As Gary threw himself down beside the body, he saw there was nothing left of it. It had been riddled, turned into a sieve. Everything inside had leaked out. The body was as flat as an empty cushion.

Here was a foxhole that Gary knew for certain was one of his – a deep hole dug beneath a boulder. Around the top of the hole was a battlement of turf. It had been a great protection during the artillery barrage – it could have taken a direct hit from an M66. For an infantryman, though, it had been dead easy. A grenade in the hole, a burst of fire, and they were well cooked.

Only after an hour, two hours, perhaps more, when they had covered no more than a few hundred yards, trench by trench, did the shells start falling ahead of them again. Kiszley could reorganize the company, ready them for another push, on for a mile more, to the end of the ridge.

We reached another foxhole, this one not blasted to bits. There were toothpaste tubes, bits of poncho torn by shrapnel and the wind, old shoes, water-bottles and a bloody bandage on the ground.

'Look at this.' Gary held up a shredded glove. 'This bloke must have been holding his grenade when he was hit and it went off.' This was probably the reason for the bloody bandage. 'Looks like they were throwing in their hands already.'

Some were, poor bastards. Down there, on the lower slopes, they were mostly conscripts, utterly unprepared for the cold, some so filthy and demoralized they were covered in their own excrement. They had had dysentery. Their clothing was caked, right up their backs. Officers and better-trained troops were up above with the snipers. Many of them fled, many surrendered. Many more would have surrendered if they'd had the time, but in the heat of battle there was no time. It's a risky business to stop, disarm, and tie and hood a prisoner. Lose the momentum of battle, and you lose the battle.

On to open grass, uphill towards the end of the main ridge, falling into shell-craters every few paces, with more exploding all around as retreating Argentinians called in artillery fire behind them – impossible to see the holes in the dark and the crazy shadows of the flares, with your eyes blinded by tracers, and flares, and star-shells.

Up ahead, silhouetted in the light of the blasts and explosions and fire-fights and distant mortar-flares, Major Kiszley was flung backwards by a burst of machine-gun fire.

'Fuck's sake!'

Everyone hit the deck, thinking they were all about to get taken out. But to their astonishment, Kiszley stood up again.

He'd taken two rounds, and should have been dead. One had lodged in his compass, the other hit the bayonet-scabbard at his waist. He got away with heavy bruising on his hips, nothing more.

'Come on!' he shouted, as if aggrieved that the others were slowing things down.

Ahead, a jumble of rocks, silhouetted by a dim orange glow. The rocks – this was as far as they had to go. Into the rocks, only nine of them left out of thirty, but the momentum was still there.

They reached the rocks, and looked over. By now, the darkness was beginning to lighten. There, for the first time, Gary saw the lights of Stanley. For the last two weeks he had seen nothing but sea and moor. Stanley had been the objective, the purpose of the battle and the war, but he'd forgotten all about it. And there it was, not blacked out, but glowing like fairy lights in the twilight. He was astonished. Gob-smacked. It was so close it looked as though they could just take it.

Not yet. A hail of fire, from another rocky redout 100 metres ahead, down the far slope. Instantly, they were back under cover of the rocks. Below, Right Flank were working their way around. Gary and his section knew what they had to do: return fire, and allow Right Flank to take the enemy out. Behind, the battle was still in progress for the higher ground. It would take another hour of fierce fighting to take it.

Exhilarated by victory and the fact of their survival, they 'went firm'. Gary picked up a GPMG and began firing down on the rocks ahead. Behind him, under cover, the others were checking their kit, re-distributing ammunition picked up from the wounded, watching cowering prisoners – some of them teenagers looking like middle-aged men, haggard with hunger, and exposure and the strain of battle. Half an hour passed. At some point, Gary and one of the others, Dalgleish, went forward to drag back a couple of Guards who had been wounded in the assault on the rocks ahead.

Daylight. On the slopes below, other Guards were working their way up, with casualties, while Argentinian troops were heading out, into the valley, and towards Stanley. Many were helping wounded or carrying casualties in stretchers. No longer targets, they went untouched.

As the noise of battle began to die along the length of the mountain, twenty or twenty-five Guards started to help the newly-bandaged wounded down the hillside to a regimental aid post. They were making their way across open ground a couple of hundred yards down, when mortar rounds exploded in and around them. A single volley, no one knew where from. Eight, nine, ten men were down, the rest diving for cover.

Gary and several others ran down to help. It was like a butcher's shop. He'd seen nothing like it. Four men dead, perhaps eight others wounded. Meat everywhere. A man simply blown to pieces. Gary was about to help one of the wounded, a skinny lad, lying unconscious. Then, more mortar rounds, not so accurate this time. The boy sat up. Gary laid him down. He sat up again. Explosions, shrapnel flying. Gary forced him down, and kept him down, almost covering him with his body. The body below him reacted again, with a powerful jerk, jack-knifing Gary off his upper body on to his legs. It was a convulsion. The boy had been dead all along.

This was different. This was not simply shocking, but outside anything that anyone should ever have to see or tolerate. Casualties, harmless men, dying for nothing, when not far away Argentinian casualties were going free. You'd think that after what he'd been through, nothing more would have touched Gary. Wrong. Now there was a real anger, personal antipathy. It wouldn't last, but right then it only needed a target to find an outlet.

Back up in the rocks, focusing again on the remaining nest of Argentinians ahead, suddenly a round smacked into a rock by Gary. A sniper, somewhere behind them.

Another round. Crack-and-thump – the crack of the bullet,

the thump of the gun firing. That gave the direction. Flash-crack-thump. Now they knew where he was, and watched for him as he fired twice more, moving between shots. Not a great marksman.

'You and you, come with me,' said Kiszley to Gary and Eddie Collins. Gary picked up his GPMG, 200 rounds of ammunition and a 66 anti-tank rocket. It wasn't hard to trace the sniper. They spotted him as he was scrambling up rocks 100 metres away. It was an easy shot. Gary had the 66 prepared. The sniper was just trying to lever himself into a better position, pushing himself up backwards on to a ledge above the cliff that cuts off Tumbledown to the north, when Gary fired. The rocket hit the guy in the thighs. His lower legs, still in their boots, plopped straight down, and the rest of him vanished up and over the cliff.

'Should have apologized really, Simon,' he said, staring up at the rocks. 'You're always supposed to say "Sorry" when you hit someone with a rocket. But I was angry.'

He returned to the end of the ridge.

Below, the Argentinians were fleeing, walking off the mountain, in a slow, random stream towards Stanley.

Today, the end of Tumbledown is capped by a memorial, a cross standing at the head of a track weaving up from the moorland. The view from the ridge now was much as Gary had seen it that dawn: over to the left, the long rise of Wireless Ridge; Stanley lying at the base of a gentle slope of drought-tinged brown grass, broken by patches of open peat – here and there black peaty pools mirroring the sky.

It had taken six hours in all. What had it felt like, really?

'In some ways, Simon, they were the best six hours of my life. I was that close to the edge. It was better than any bird I've ever had, better than any car I've ever driven. Up there, I decided who lived and who died. I was God. That's how it felt.'

Now, that's a truth, and soldiers know it. But I'd never heard it said with such power and honesty.

There are other answers, longer-term ones, and he gave me these, too. He did what he had to do, but he was scarred by the experience. Like me, he had survived, while others had died. Both of us felt the wound of guilt. But unlike me in another way, he felt that perhaps his craziness that night had led others to their deaths.

I would say the opposite. I'd say that perhaps his craziness was the greatest sanity, and that by fighting well and leading well, he had saved lives.

But then, he'll never know, and the guilt will never completely heal.

13

WIRELESS RIDGE

2 December 1991

While Gary was waiting in the pool of silence and darkness in the lee of Goat Ridge for Tumbledown to begin, John was waiting to start the fight for Wireless Ridge. He described his experience of the battle as we walked together up the rough flank of the ridge from Moody Brook, the stream that separates Wireless Ridge from Tumbledown, then along the peaty, rocky crest.

He and his platoon had been lifted over by helicopter, to assemble behind Mount Kent. During the assaults on Harriet, Longdon and Two Sisters, 2 Para tabbed around Kent to the back of Longdon, while senior officers checked the next objective, Wireless Ridge.

In fact, the ridge was two ridges: one to the north, out of sight of Stanley, and one that runs along the far side of Stanley Harbour – a five-mile rise that begins opposite Tumbledown and ends beyond Stanley itself. Other companies of 2 Para were to seize the northern section; 'D' Company, including John's 12 Platoon, were to take the ridge fringeing the harbour.

The mood was very different from the build-up to Goose

Green. Then, the lads were ignorant. Now, they were veterans. They knew it would be a hard fight, knew there would be a lot of bullets coming their way. John offered no false hopes, telling his lads coldly that some of them would not be coming back, and that the best way to ensure survival was to remember what they'd been taught. Here, if anywhere, the enemy would make a stand. It was the last defence before Stanley. If Wireless Ridge went, the war was as good as over.

Because of their experience at Goose Green, some of the men were more apprehensive, and some thought it was unfair to impose on them a second time when they were meant to be a reserve battalion – 'Let someone else have a go.'

'Shut up, you lot. We were reserve before. It makes no difference.'

Besides, almost all of them had bad feet, with open sores still unhealed from the marches over the Sussex Mountains. It was a painful business squeezing on damp boots a size or more too small for their cracked and swollen feet.

They drew some strength from the knowledge that the far end of the ridge was to be taken by 'friendly forces', which they knew could only mean the SAS. For this reason the Paras were to stop advancing when they reached a line of telegraph poles across the ridge near the end of the estuary.

Waiting to start, a bitter wind froze all of them as they stood or sat, loaded down with the usual sixty pounds of ammunition. Some of them kicked rocks to work some feeling back into their numbed feet.

As soon as movement began across the start line, the cold was forgotten. The effort of carrying ammunition and weapons uphill, and the flow of adrenalin made you forget everything except the moment. This time there was no attempt to disguise the advance. Artillery shells began to blast the rocky heights, and flares – 'illum' – lit the whole area. The gunners had pre-recorded all Argentinian positions, and every company had an FOO (forward observation officer) to report the advance by radio and ensure that the supporting barrage was always landing a 'bound' – 250 metres – ahead.

Up ahead, silhouetted by artillery blasts, was the ridge, but with no real opposition yet. At one point, though, an artillery round landed nearby. John happened to be close to a young private, the medic, Jerry Godfrey. A piece of red-hot shrapnel whanged off a rock, and whizzed through the sleeve of Godfrey's windproof. Both of them dived for cover, with John on top. As they got up, Godfrey wiped his hands over his face in relief. 'That was close,' he muttered. Then his expression changed, and he sniffed. Argentinians had used the place as a latrine. His hands had been covered with excrement. So now, too, was his face.

'God!' said John. 'You'll be the death of us! Get away! Go and collect some two-inch mortar rounds!'

They climbed the ridge, and began to work their way along it. Still no opposition. A bunker off to the right, down in the valley, looked as if it was abandoned. John sent off two lads to check.

At first John's twenty men were close to two other platoons, 10 and 11, but somehow his lot were already moving faster than the others. Up ahead was a fortress of rock, silhouetted in the light of the flares. It was a natural defence, and everyone advanced warily, expecting fire.

To his surprise, nothing. The rocks were abandoned. The Argentinians had pulled out in a hurry, perhaps at the sight of the British advance, perhaps due to the artillery. They had left their radio sets behind, still switched on.

12 Platoon emerged from the rocks, and for the first time saw the full range of the darkened valley, Moody Brook below, flashes and explosions from the flanks of Tumbledown, and in the distance, a sudden brilliance.

'Sarge, look! The lights are on in Stanley!'

'Shut up, and keep moving.' John was more interested in the tail-lights of vehicles he could see down on the floor of the valley.

John turned back briefly to shepherd in the lads he'd sent off to clear the bunker, and eased forward again to rejoin the rest of the platoon. Overhead was the reassuring rush of friendly artillery shells, crashing down on the ridge ahead.

At this moment, however, hell broke loose. The noise of the shells overhead was suddenly different, not a whoosh, but an ominous whistle. They were falling short. John threw himself down, and hoped. Six rounds, a barrage from all six guns, landed together, among the group, exploding in the rocks with a fury of shrapnel and rock fragments.

As the noise died, John heard his company commander, Major Philip Neame, going mad with the FOO, telling him in the most vivid terms what he could do with his guns. Someone, somewhere, had blundered, seriously, because on the other side of the rocks a man was killed and another injured.

It took an hour to re-range the guns, while the Paras waited in the shelter of the rocks.

Once this was sorted out, they moved on over open ground towards a second mass of rocks. The artillery barrage was now steady again, but the rocks some 200 yards ahead presented a formidable obstacle. They poked up through the top of the ridge in a cluster of pinnacles, like some crazy castle with a motley collection of turrets and battlements.

Out there in the open there was no good cover. As soon as John and his men walked out of the rocks, down the soft grassy slope, flares burst overhead. They were clear as targets in a fairground.

A shout in Spanish, then a curtain of fire came at them from the rocks.

Instantly, the men hit the deck, finding whatever cover they could – low stones, clumps of earth, tiny dips in the peat.

John knew that they had to move, and yelled for them to get their heads up and return fire, force the enemy down, create a lull for a further advance. Risking himself, he ran, bent double, to the closest men, shouting at them to return fire.

It was a classic infantryman's nightmare: to return fire, they had to put themselves in view of the enemy, with flares drifting down overhead, creating a strange scene of shifting shadows, and with rounds zipping overhead and smacking into the soil.

Within a few minutes, as men realized that they had survived the onslaught, they peeked above their cover long enough to aim and fire. John led half a dozen men forward. Right by them was a pond, a pit of black. The lads ran round to either side, still in the open, heading across the flat ground to a little rise hardly visible except as a dark shadow cast by the flares.

They threw themselves down again, aimed, fired, stood, then on another fifty yards towards the base of the rocks. Once there, John knew, they would be on equal footing with the Argentinians.

He looked back. There was a body on the ground.

New orders: flares from the two-inch mortar, fire at any positions the men could see, identify the next piece of cover, and then, as soon as the flare faded into darkness, two men – Jerry Godfrey, the medic, was one of them – to run back and drag in the man who was down.

It was Fred Slough, badly hit, barely conscious. He had a bullet through the head. Godfrey began to patch him up. For some reason, Fred tried to tear the bandages off. He also had a chest wound, but they didn't see that till later.

Within minutes, the sergeant major, summoned over the radio, was up with them, organizing Godfrey and three others, one from another platoon, to act as stretcher-bearers. They headed back, doubled over, hitting the deck with each artillery burst, until they vanished in the rocks behind.

Fred survived until he reached hospital, but died later, the only casualty to die while in the expert hands of the Army medics.

Sixteen men left.

Meanwhile, John had sent Gosling and Spencer to one

side to clear another bunker just down from the top of the ridge.

Though reduced, the platoon was in with a good chance now. They were well protected by rock. By firing flares, they could see where the Argentinians were, and spot the next piece of cover. As the light died, eight kept firing, while the others ran forward. Then, when they were 'firm', they could do the same for their comrades.

A couple of such pepperpotting manoeuvres, and they were deep enough into the rocks to use grenades to take out individual positions. The results were still there to see — rocks shattered and scarred, exposing pink bits beneath the outer covering of grey.

Fighting forward, the Paras now found positions manned only by the dead and wounded. No one bothered with the wounded. In the heat of action, as John had told his men, it was often too dangerous to look after your own wounded — better to return for them later, when you've secured your position — so Argentinian wounded were simply disarmed, if they were lucky, and left unattended until after the battle.

The able-bodied Argentinians had retreated along the ridge, and then downhill towards Stanley, leaving the mess of two months of occupation: ponchos, toothpaste tubes, bottles, food (especially tins of bully beef), clothing, all peppered by shrapnel. It was all still there when John and I walked the ridge together, along with a pile of cow-bones marking a kitchen area and communication wires for field telephones snaking away to the company HQ further along the ridge, tucked down on the Stanley side.

John returned over the open ground to find the other two, who should have been back from clearing the bunker. He was surprised to find Major Neame standing on his own, with his radio, controlling the artillery. Neame was slight in build, but large in personality: calm, clear-thinking, quiet, dry sense of humour, always a move ahead, always visible, always accessible, and always ready to let his subordinates get on with the job. Wherever the action was thickest, that's where he would be. Good man.

'Hello, Meredith,' he said. 'What's up?'

John explained about the two he was looking for, then asked: 'Where's the rest of your headquarters, sir?' Neame should have had radio operators and the FOO with him.

'Oh, I've lost them somewhere.'

'Where's 10 Platoon, then?'

'They should be on your left, Meredith.'

'Well, there's nobody there, sir,' said John, and moved on.

He had just spotted his two lost sheep coming up the slope towards him when he heard raised voices from behind a nearby rock. Two of 10 Platoon's NCOs were arguing about whether they should be advancing or not. One was saying he'd been told to go forward by the platoon commander; the other replied: 'Well, I'm not moving until he comes and tells me.'

John stepped round the corner, and ordered them both forcefully to move up right now, and stop leaving 12 Platoon's flank exposed.

'See,' said the first as they hurried off. 'Told you.'

John collected the two privates, and returned to his own platoon, still safely in the rocky fortress.

Minutes later, they were out of the rocks, advancing over open grass, because suddenly there were no more enemy troops, and they were at the line of poles that marked their objective. Below them, the lights of Stanley glowed. They couldn't go any further without risking an encounter with the SAS, who were supposed to be advancing from the opposite direction.

It wasn't over yet. There were still bullets coming in from Tumbledown, and a few from snipers who had been bypassed in the rush forward. Bullets and glowing pieces of shrapnel zipped overhead, smacked into the grass or ricocheted off rocks.

John took shelter behind a rock. In the lull, he became aware of new sounds, shouts from over the edge of the ridge, down towards Moody Brook.

'Minnock!' John shouted across to a gunner who had a decent view. 'What can you see down there?'

A pause, then: 'I can't see anything, Sergeant.'

'Use your night-sights, dimwit.'

Another pause. 'Christ! There's hundreds of them!'

Some of the more determined Argentinians had launched a counter-attack up the hill from Moody Brook, right towards the Paras. It turned out that this counter-attack, one of the bravest actions in the war, was launched not by the regulars who had fled from the ridge, but by armoured car crewmen, from the vehicles John had seen earlier, followed by members of another company based on the lower slopes of Tumbledown, perhaps 150 men in all. There seemed to be three waves to the attack, one of which actually got within grenade range. ('Cheek!' said John, remembering.)

Fortunately, they were inexperienced, and fighting uphill, and knew the war was nearly lost. Perhaps it was to stimulate their morale that they had been shouting on the way up. That had only served to give away their position.

The 16 Paras, using four machine guns, and calling in artillery, fought off the attack in less than half an hour, without loss or injury to anyone. The only consequence was that a couple of snipers managed to sneak into the rocks through which the Paras had come earlier.

The battle died again. Still the tracers and Argentinian artillery shells were coming in. John told Gosling he could shelter behind his rock, while he himself settled into a shell-crater with Jonathan Page, company commander since Jim Barry's death, safe from the fizz and zip of snipers' bullets and shrapnel.

He had been there only a few minutes when a shadow loomed up above him. It was Neame, walking forward to check progress at first hand.

'How's it going, Meredith?' he asked in his usual casual way, as if out for a Sunday afternoon stroll.

'Fuck off, sir,' said John. 'You're attracting fire.'

'Oh, OK then, Meredith,' Neame replied mildly, and wandered away.

Perhaps it was Neame's inspiration, for not long afterwards Jonathan Page remarked: 'I'll go and check the soldiers.'

'The soldiers are all right,' John said. 'They're all in good positions. Leave them.'

'Well, I'll go and check them anyway.'

'OK, but crawl.'

'No, I'll be all right,' Page said, and stepped out of the hole. He must have been neatly silhouetted against the background, because he took three paces, and *bang*, over he went, hit by a sniper over in the rocks behind them.

Knights, the signaller, ran over, and checked Page for wounds. 'I can't feel any blood, sir. Where are you hit?'

'In the side.'

A pause. 'There's no blood. There's nothing wrong with you.'

It was true. The round had gone through his ammunition pouch, between two grenades, hit a magazine, bent all the rounds, and been deflected straight back out. Page had a massive bruise, but nothing more. Why on earth Neame wasn't picked off, John couldn't imagine.

There was nothing else to do. As dawn broke, it became clear that Tumbledown had been taken. Sniper fire from there died. The snipers in the rocks back down Wireless Ridge had been taken out or captured by other platoons. John and Jonathan Page climbed out of their shell-hole.

John walked forward to the brow of the ridge. The view looked then much as it did when we were there together. Directly below, the remains of a Marine barracks, with one of the few trees on the island. The estuary stretched away to the left, with a rough, single-track road leading along the coast to Stanley two miles away; to the right, Tumbledown, the slope punctuated by a single farmhouse.

Argentinian troops were streaming slowly off the mountain opposite, and around the head of the estuary. If the Paras had been allowed to work further forward and then cut down to the estuary, they would have trapped hundreds more on the peninsula. They could have done it, too, because the SAS never turned up – they had been driven off before they even landed.

John led me down the slope, round the edge of a rock buttress. Here was a strong position, probably the HQ. Piles of beer cans. Ammunition boxes. Some old wheels from a 120mm mortar, probably slung off the upper slopes by an eager Para. Its toolbox had a shrapnel hole torn through it.

'I wouldn't like to have assaulted this,' I said.

'Nor would I. They were well set up here. They didn't seem to be short of anything. If we'd been up here, we'd have died of old age before giving up.'

For John's sixteen remaining men, the battle was over. They had performed well: superb close-quarter fighting, with only light casualties, had led to a victory that included the defeat of the only counter-attack during the whole assault. Together with Tumbledown, Wireless Ridge had unlocked the road to Stanley – and to Argentinian surrender. Afterwards, the only sour note was – and still is – that John's commanding officer, Phil Neame, was not decorated, an omission that reflected both on the man and on those under him.

As daylight strengthened, as the noise of battle died over on Tumbledown, the Paras were ordered back along the ridge, and then down the hillside, taking a roundabout route to avoid possible mine-fields.

They were down on the road by Moody Brook when new orders came through: 'Move in fifteen minutes. They've surrendered.'

The helmets came off, the berets went on, and 2 Para tabbed on into Stanley.

14

AN END AND A NEW BEGINNING

The trip, the stresses, the dramas, were over. On the last day, everyone else went off to look at penguins. I was happy to pack, wander round Stanley, and think over what had happened.

Then the next morning we were off, out to MPA for the RAF flight home. It was misty, and there was talk of the flight being delayed. I didn't care. We would leave eventually.

As it turned out, the mist lifted, and we left on time. There was a bit of excitement when two RAF Phantoms settled a few feet from our wing-tips, accompanying us out of Falklands air space, then flicking off to right and left with a roar.

I fell into a dreamy stupor. The last time I made that trip, I had been in a haze of drugs and pain, but nothing of that came back. The past, and its memories, were falling away behind me.

I had been away three weeks. Only three weeks, but enough to change my life yet again.

The burden of the past had begun to slip away from the moment I shook Carlos's hand. Nothing else could equal the effect of that, but everything I had experienced afterwards removed yet another part of the burden. I had had more than my share of stress and emotion, but Gary and John had laughed me through the hard times. 'What's up with you?' Gary asked, the morning after the barmaid had a go at me. 'You look like you've combed your hair with a thunder-flash.' More than that, they had opened their past to me, and brought it alive.

As a result, there was one source of grieving I could escape from: the feeling that I had missed out, that there was another life that I had never lived – the life I had planned for myself – and the war I had never had a chance to fight. Now I came to think about it more deeply, I realized there was nothing here to grieve over after all.

For one thing, I would not have experienced much of the war even if I hadn't been burned. I would have been stuck in a trench with the other Welsh Guards until the Argentinians surrendered.

For another, I now understood better what war meant, and knew beyond doubt, more strongly than ever, that I would not have wanted to go through it. As Gary and John said, they took boys into war, and brought men out. But that maturity, that loss of innocence, was achieved at a terrible cost. There was a lot of horror there, a lot of sights and sounds that may change you but can't possibly be called *good*. I would never have wanted to kill, or risk death in action, or see mates die like that. You can see the effects on men who have been through a battle – the '1,000-yard stare', the look that has seen fearful things, the look that is always waiting to cloud the gaze of otherwise ordinary men. I had had the great good fortune to feel the fear and dreadful exhilaration of close-quarter warfare at second hand, and thanked my lucky stars I would never have to see it for myself. I never had to play God, with the power of life and death in my trigger-finger. That was a life I was glad I had not lived.

The more I thought about what the bomb meant, the stranger it all became. All anger at Carlos had disappeared. I had never thought I would blame him or hate him personally for what happened, but there had been a lot of anger stored up. I had felt it when I met him. Now it just wasn't there any more.

If he wasn't to blame, if no one was to blame, if there was no cause for anger, it seemed to me that somehow the whole thing was fated. I was fated to get injured. This thought reminded me of something that had happened on the *QE2* on the way down. We were watching a horror movie – one of the *Damien* films, I think. That was odd, because I never watched horror movies. For some reason, they bored me. Anyway, someone in the film lifted Damien's hair and found the mark of the Devil: 666, the treble six. It occurred to me then that our British Forces post office box number was 666, and I had this peculiar feeling that something terrible was going to happen.

If it was fate, then perhaps I would have got injured anyway. It's hard to imagine how, because the Welsh Guards weren't involved in the fighting. But one bloke did get killed by shell-fire on the night of 13 June, and several of the lads were injured when a Sidewinder missile malfunctioned. Perhaps, if I'd been there, I'd have been hit by a shell or blown up.

If that was a possibility that awaited me, perhaps being hit by Carlos's bomb actually saved me from something worse.

Certainly it gave me something better than I might have had. Because of the bomb, my life changed. I suffered – I'm permanently scarred – but still my future opened up in ways that would never have been possible if I had remained a Welsh Guard squaddie: the documentaries; the first book; this book; the charities; the radio; and above all Lucy and James, who were there at Brize Norton to pick me up with my Mam.

I would never have met Lucy without Carlos. Without Carlos, there would be no James.

It was great to be back, to hold Lucy, hold James, to see how much he'd grown, and know there was nothing left from the past to darken our lives together.

I have no idea yet what I'm going to do with my future, but whatever it holds, it will be for the three of us together, and I know I'm free to seize it – and enjoy it.